TREASURE FOUND

BY CINTHIA JAMES

Book design by Cinthia James
Artwork by Cinthia James

ISBN 978-3-00-074429-7 (paperback)
ISBN 978-3-00-074430-3 (ebook)

www.cinthiajames.com

www.instagram.com/ataleof_art/

www.linkedin.com/in/cinthia-james/

DEDICATION

I...

...dedicate this book to my friends and family, especially to my Oma and Opa.

Ich...

...widme dieses Buch meinen Freunden und meiner Familie, insbesondere meiner Oma und meinem Opa.

›CONTENTS

1

2

›INTRODUCTION

This book offers a glimpse into how I found fulfillment, purpose, and joy – my own personal treasure – by creating vibrant, colorful patterns and illustrations. My journey draws inspiration from fashion, art, entertainment, and eight South Korean inter-dimensional, time traveling space pirates known as ATEEZ, whose beautiful music and conceptual art has helped me navigate the rough seas of self-doubt.

On my treasure hunt I have strengthened my conceptual thinking, created a process of finding inspiration, and developed personal projects to hone my skills in a consistent and disciplined manner. Creative ideas can come from many sources and can vary depending on your art and design destinations.

From movies, fashion, music, art, travel, and beyond, there is no shortage of inspiration to help generate a creative idea.

But where does one start and what should one create? I often ask myself,
WHAT DO I LIKE?
WHAT INSPIRES ME?

Frequently, my answers started with a process of deduction of what I don't like and what I don't want to do, helping me to narrow in on **WHAT I LOVE.**

I began by looking at images and collecting the ones I felt a connection with. I gave myself a rule of only taking pictures or buying images that really moved me.

I did have something of an advantage here, as I am a lover of art books and have been collecting them ever since my graphic design studies in San Francisco.

So, my first stop was my mini library and for you, it might be the books you collect, the magazines you read, the images you hang on your walls, the color palettes, textures and patterns throughout your home or the clothes you wear.

TAKE A LOOK AND SEE WHAT STANDS OUT TO YOU. DO YOU SEE A CONSISTENT THEME, SIMILAR SUBJECT MATTER, OR REPEATED COLOR PALETTES?

When I started looking at what I was collecting on my bookshelf, I saw a lot of fashion, pattern, and illustration, some of it on the naive side.

It became clear to me that I must truly like those things, even though I wasn't actually creating fashion art or pattern design back then.

I had tried and given up a few times on both fashion illustration and pattern design due to my lack of consistency and art classes that left me feeling like I had the largest mountain to climb; but here it was in front of me again, showing me what I gravitate to and what I truly would love to create.

It was clear that I needed to explore pattern and fashion art further, but I was still not fully convinced, so I decided to see if trips to museums and exhibitions would bring me further revelations. I took pictures of artworks that spoke to me, and I also bought fashion and home decor magazines to see what else would grab my attention.

I also gathered images on my travels and trips in nature. I collected street art, pictures of architecture, posters, and so on.

I am uncertain if at this time I was still trying to find out what I wanted to create or convince myself that it was not fashion or pattern related.

With the images I gathered there was a clear theme: pattern design, illustrated figures, and portraits.

This became my foundation. From there, I began to search for ideas and guidance from other creatives that I looked up to.

I discovered the importance of a consistent practice of drawing regularly, and developing ideas around personal projects that could help me strengthen my skills.

I came up with a few project ideas and set sail with two. One was perfume illustrations and the other was creating fashion art and illustrations inspired by K-pop music videos.

I called this venture *A Tale of K-pop* and my greatest inspiration was ATEEZ, the South Korean boy band with a pirate concept.

The perfume illustrations couldn't hold my attention for long, and my K-pop art became more like fan art, focused on the idols (artists) themselves.

I felt I had veered away from my original plan, but I still enjoyed drawing my idols because it was clear evidence of the progress I was making with a consistent drawing practice.

My art started to evolve. I began to add color and pattern designs, and to create my own characters. I decided to change my project name from *A Tale of K-pop* to *A Tale of Art.*

With the evolution of my project, I continued to draw K-pop idols and gained a lot of inspiration from their music videos. Throughout it all, a consistent source of inspiration was – and still is – ATEEZ, the inter-dimensional space pirates.

For their first anniversary since their debut, I decided to create illustrations inspired by each of their music videos from that time. Looking back at these old illustrations makes me cringe, but also shows me that I have progressed so much.

IN THIS BOOK I WOULD LIKE TO SHARE WITH YOU MY PROCESS AND SOME OF MY ART, WITH THE HOPE THAT IT WILL BE A GUIDE OR AN INSPIRATION THAT MIGHT SPARK YOUR OWN CREATIVE JOURNEY.

Images: *Liquid Courage*, perfume art with motivational words

Courage

Individual

Balance

CREATIVE

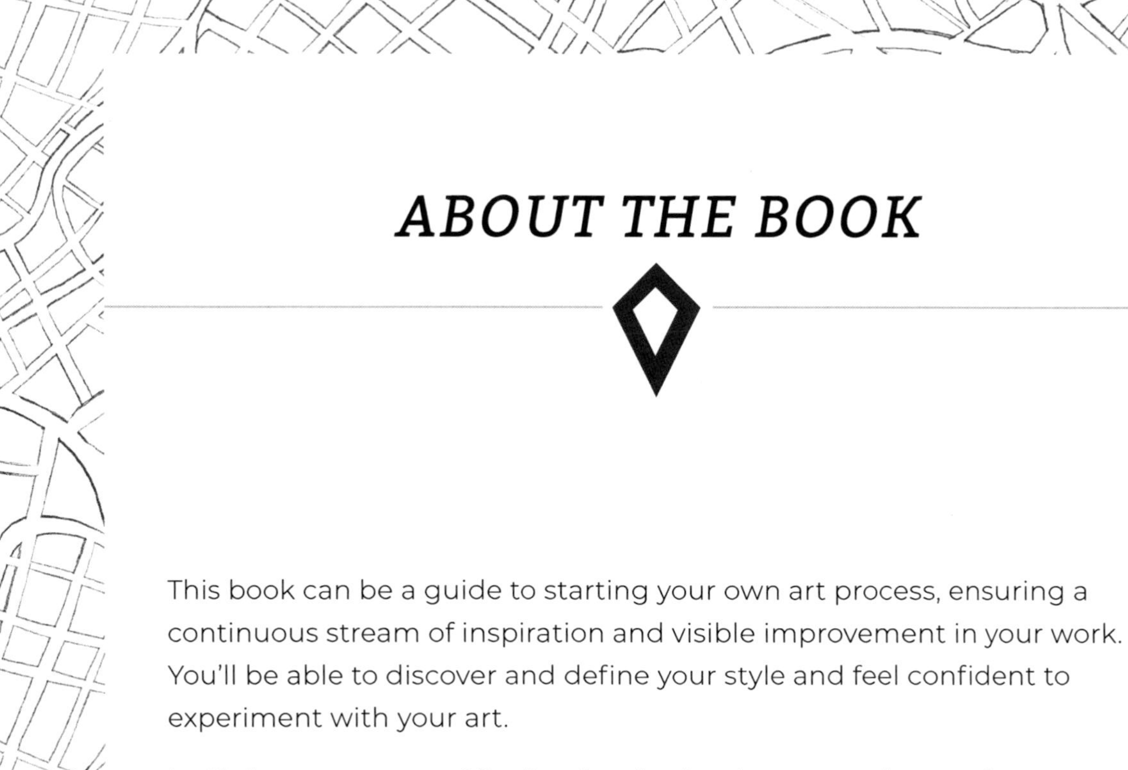

ABOUT THE BOOK

This book can be a guide to starting your own art process, ensuring a continuous stream of inspiration and visible improvement in your work. You'll be able to discover and define your style and feel confident to experiment with your art.

I will show you ways of finding inspiration, how to understand art as a discipline, and I'll outline some design fundamentals.

My inspiration for the visual art in the book is a combination of ATEEZ's music and visual concept, fashion, entertainment, and the world around me.

In each section, you will see that sometimes the artworks present visual examples for the topic being discussed or represent final pieces that decorate the chapters. Depending on the artwork shown, the piece could either have followed the creation process as a whole or used key steps in the process, such as reworking and reimagining.

You might find yourself returning to certain sections in the book and trying out or adapting the ideas to assist you in your workflow.

I hope that the book inspires and guides you in your creative journey.

1
BEGINNING WITH THE
BASICS

WHAT GRAPHIC DESIGN TAUGHT ME

Though in my art journey I have moved towards illustration rather than focusing on the visual narrative of my graphic design studies, I still follow some key fundamentals that help me find inspiration, focus my ideas, and ensure consistency in my art practice and quality of work.

IN THIS SECTION, I HIGHLIGHT THE FUNDAMENTALS THAT I RETURN TO REGULARLY.

There are times when I create something that doesn't require a lot of consideration, but when I want to create a series of work or push my learning, I go back to the basics.

LIMITATION
BREEDS CREATIVITY

Even if you have the biggest budget in the world and full freedom to create something, it can be beneficial to add some constraints on your ideas to sharpen your focus and push your creativity.

I FIND THAT LIMITING COLORS, CONCEPT, STYLE, AND ELEMENTS ON THE PAGE HELPS ME FOCUS ON THE MESSAGE AND MY AUDIENCE.

The limitations push you to think of what is possible in conveying meaning, whether your own expression or a client's message.

STORYTELLING

CREATING AN IDEA

Working with a narrative in your artwork helps you tell a broader story and convey your ideas visually.

CLEAR AND CONSIDERED NARRATIVES CREATE NUANCE. THIS MAKES VIEWERS OF YOUR WORK COME BACK TO ENJOY ALL THE DETAILS.

It also makes them want to know more about the behind-the-scenes process of how the artwork came to be.

So, what story is your art telling or what creative idea are you trying to convey?

›COMPONENTS

BREAK PROJECTS INTO COMPONENTS

As creatives, working out where to start can sometimes feel overwhelming, especially if we have ideas or projects in mind that involve activities or skills we haven't tried yet.

USING THIS PRINCIPLE, YOU WORK BACKWARDS, BREAKING THE PROJECT DOWN INTO ITS SMALLER COMPONENTS.

Then you can create a plan for each component, develop a timeline for how everything fits together, and record what you learn from each activity. This process leads to a fruitful practice.

BLACK & WHITE

IF IT WORKS IN BLACK AND WHITE, IT WORKS IN COLOR

THIS IS WHERE SKETCHING, CREATING INK VERSIONS, OR COLORING DIGITAL WORK IN BLACK AND WHITE COME INTO PLAY.

No matter how colorful or intricate you would like your final artwork to be, creating a black-and-white version of your piece can help you determine whether the work is balanced and if the eye moves freely when viewing it.

›NEW WORK
CREATE CONSISTENTLY

KEEP YOUR PORTFOLIO UP TO DATE BY ADDING NEW WORK REGULARLY.

I'm not a huge believer in drawing every day, but a regular habit of drawing multiple times a week has worked for me.

Following a plan, with a consistent source of inspiration, and practical strategies to harness that inspiration ensures you will create work and update your portfolio often.

STYLE
VS CONCEPT

STYLE is the way an idea is expressed or how a subject is presented. We all have an innate style or a way of representing meaning in our work, and with experimentation and personal projects, we can explore and refine how that style represents us through our art.

A design begins with a **CONCEPT.** This is the foundation – a visual solution for the idea that can be literal or abstract. A concept is the core of telling visual stories.

For example, the terms "movement" and "pirates" might be the concepts. In both instances, a ship might be a part of the design idea.

The concepts can be expressed in many styles: modern, baroque, fantasy, punk, bold, vibrant, whimsical – the list could go on.

I've highlighted the differences between style and concept because:

- Concepts can help you identify your style
- Concepts can help you explore various styles
- Style can bring your concept to life

When you have a strong foundation (idea) you can experiment with various styles in the same art piece or series you decide to create.

THE GRID

In its basic form, a **GRID** helps you organize and align elements that you want to have in your artwork.

Our mind and eyes naturally seek out order and patterns, and a grid can help you achieve order even in the most detailed artwork.

Grids should be seen as guidelines that support your work, not something that obstructs or confines it.

GRIDS CAN BE BROKEN.

I especially love using grids in my pattern design. When I started taking courses in surface pattern, I was often taught to create motifs and then place them randomly until it felt balanced.

Having already completed a graphic design degree, I struggled to find balance while placing motifs randomly on a page. It resulted in designs that were extremely busy and had far too many elements for my liking.

I THOUGHT TO MYSELF, WHY IS NO-ONE TALKING ABOUT GRIDS?

As a fan of the pioneering Wiener Werkstätte (Vienna Workshop), I remembered seeing some textile work by one its founders, Josef Hoffmann, which used pencil-lined grids.

He illustrated his final work on top of grids, conveying movement and energy. After viewing his designs again, I decided to use grids in my pattern work.

GRIDS
WHY I USE THEM

HIERARCHY

The grid helps to place and group elements on a page to improve visual hierarchy, allowing the eye to move from the most important to the least important elements. It also helps create a sense of balance.

NEGATIVE SPACE

Also known as "white space," negative space can be used to place visual elements in order to allow the eye to rest before taking in more information.

Negative space should be seen as a part of the overall image. There are also many artists that play with negative space, deliberately leaving out elements so that the eye and mind subconsciously create what is not present on the page.

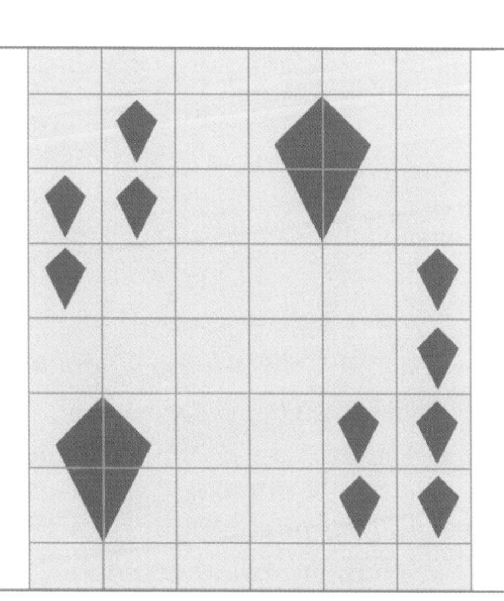

COMPOSITION

The grid can help you create a visually appealing composition.

Whenever I've struggled to create an interesting layout, I find an artwork with a composition that inspires me and create grids over the top. In this way, I can better understand how the layout of the piece is structured. For example, are the elements more to the left or the right?

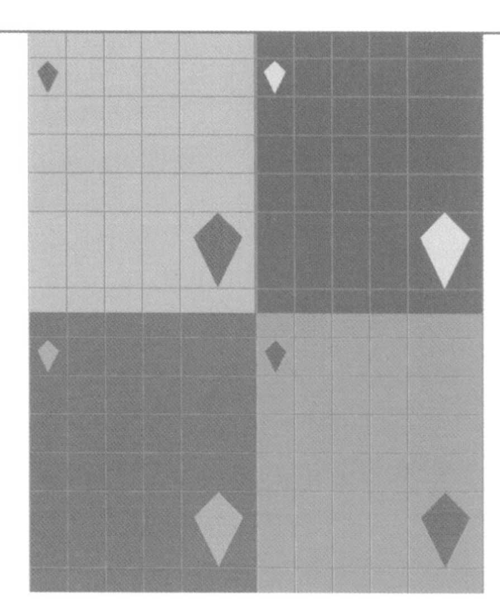

CONSISTENCY

If you are creating work in a series or planning on creating a book or zine, a grid is a must.

Look at any book or magazine you have – the page numbers and certain other elements repeat on each page in the same position. This consistency supports the viewer or reader because they know where to find the repeated information, and they can visually skip over it, if they choose, in order to focus elsewhere.

GRIDS
MODULAR GRID—RULE OF THIRDS

The most commonly known and used grid is a **MODULAR GRID.**

It is a structure that arranges elements in rows and columns that are aligned both horizontally and vertically.

You can use a nine-squared modular grid to create a composition according to the **RULE OF THIRDS**. The page is divided into thirds both horizontally and vertically creating a grid of nine squares, or "tiles."

This composition grid is easy to apply and helps in drawing viewers' attention to the subject of an image, by placing key elements on the intersecting lines.

THE RULE OF THIRDS SUPPORTS WITH HIERARCHY, NEGATIVE SPACE, AND THE OVERALL COMPOSITION.

I use modular grids and the rule of thirds in most of my art, especially in my pattern design. Both tools are simple guides that can help balance out your work.

The rule of thirds can be used to evenly place elements in a pattern tile, allowing for some of those elements to cross the intersecting lines in different ways.

This composition grid can also support with the following when designing a pattern:

- Designing complex patterns with multiple elements and layers
- Evening out negative space and creating a harmonious repeat
- Experiment with clustering
- Creating various groups of elements

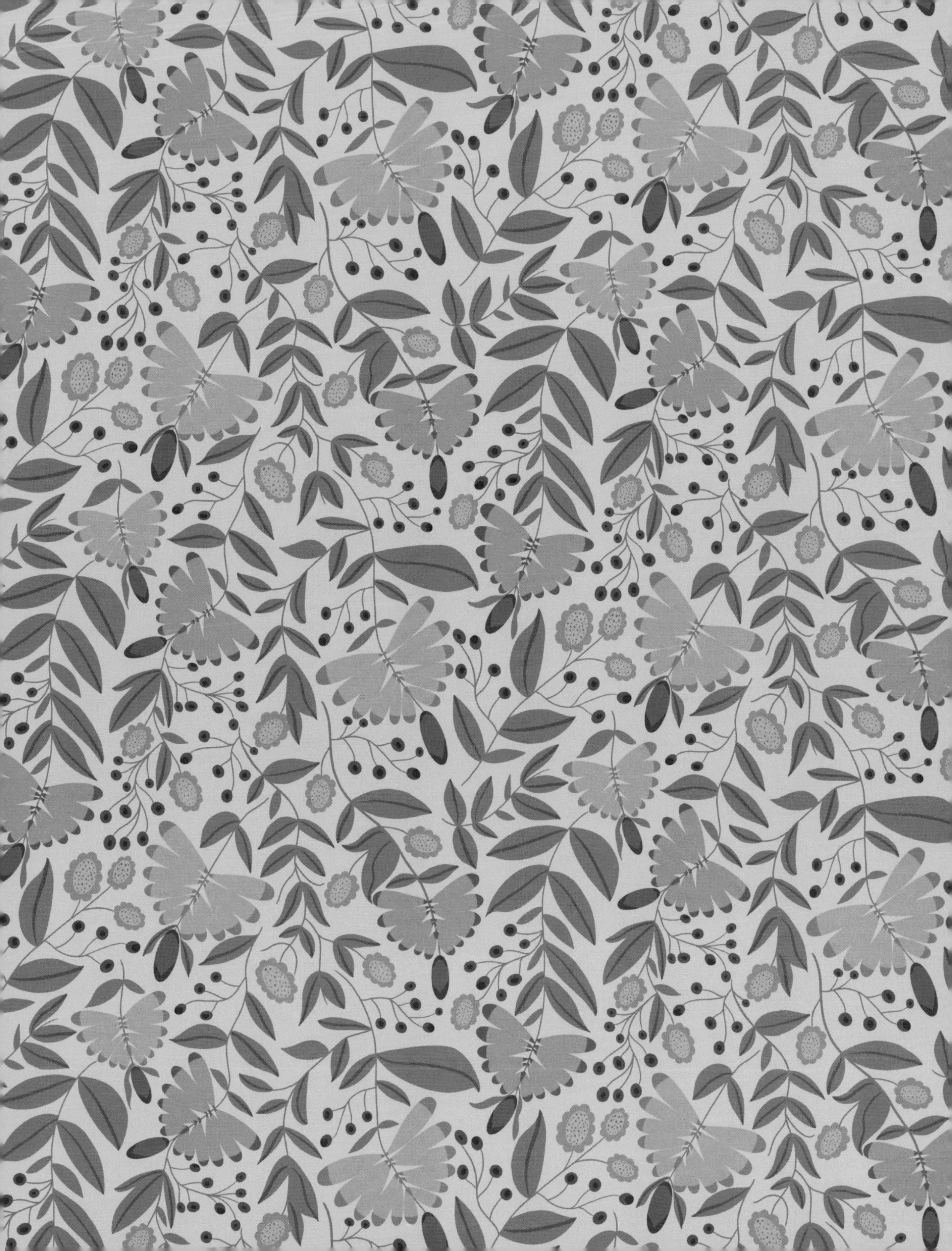

2
SEARCHING FOR
INSPIRATION

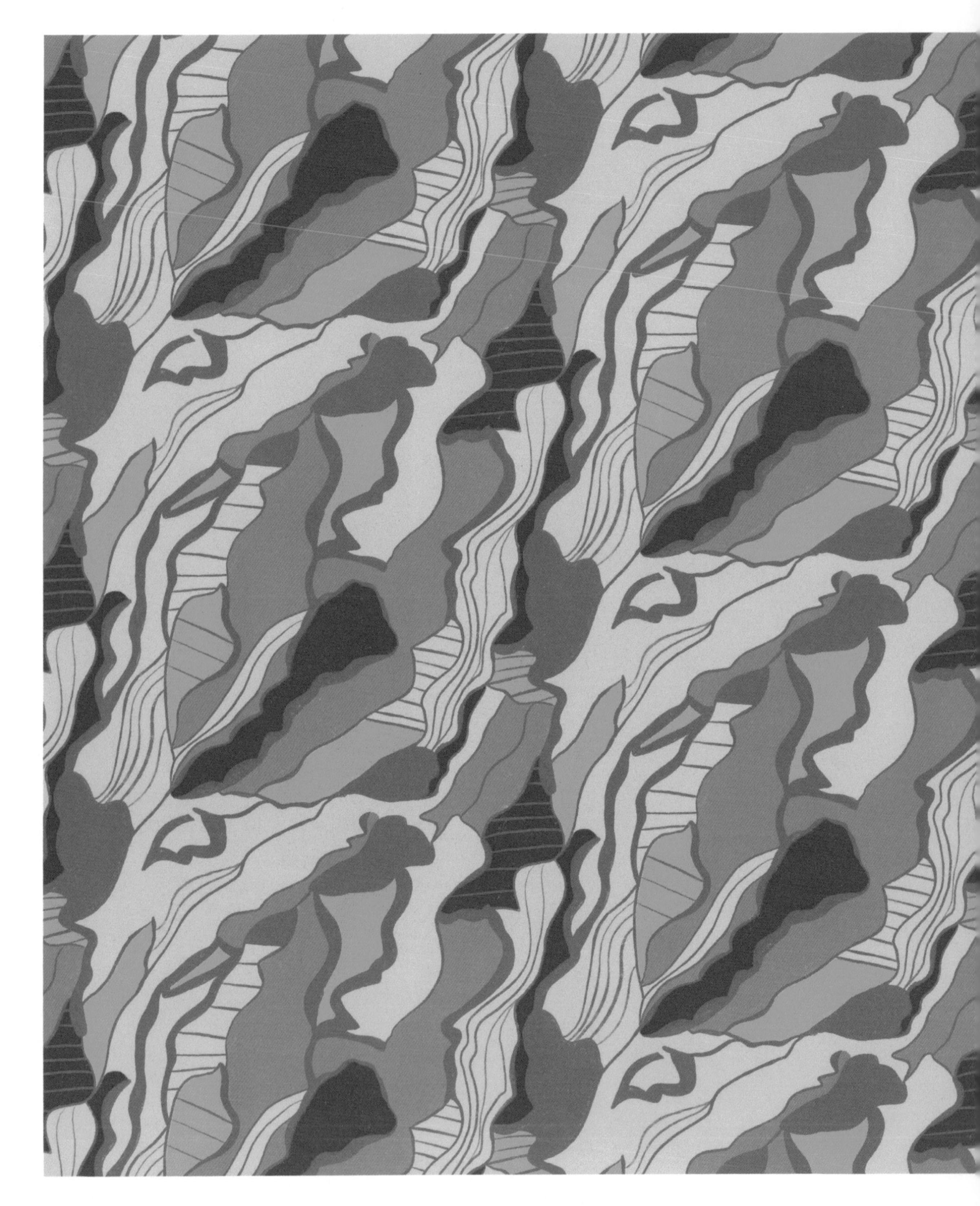

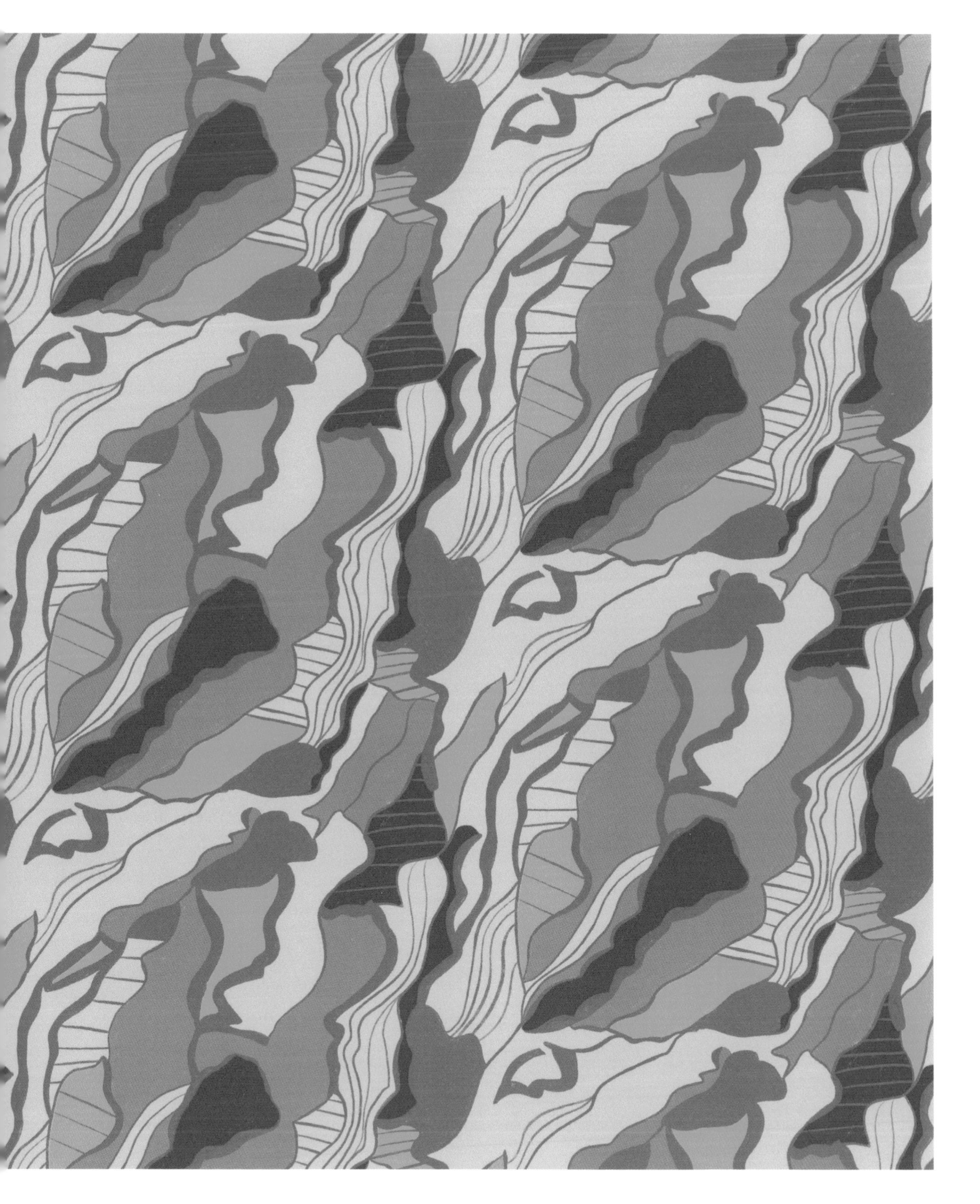

INSPIRATION
VS INFLUENCE

I have come to see **INFLUENCE** as something that has more of a lasting effect. It refers to the activities you do and the people you look up to that impact the way you create your art.

For instance, my favorite painter is Gustav Klimt. I have been told that my pattern designs and illustrations sometimes show that I am influenced by his work and the Wiener Werkstätte as a whole.

In some of my patterns you can see the influence of the "in between" of Art Deco and Art Nouveau.

As a huge fan of the Wiener Werkstätte, I look at their work often, which creates a visual memory that I draw from.

I also love the works of Alexander Girard, who had more of a bold, graphic style. These influences, plus my natural hand, generate the art I create.

My love of pattern was originally influenced by my grandmother and the way her home is decorated.

I didn't pay much attention to my Oma's home decor until I decided to create my own patterns. Seemingly in an instant, I could see all the patterns around me, on the furnishings, the walls, and so on.

INSPIRATION is a bit more immediate. It can relate to an emotion and/or an idea to create something specific. It is where your influence gets molded, based on your current situation or circumstances.

Inspiration also changes more rapidly. It's sometimes the spark you need to put pencil to paper.

Think about who and what has influenced you and your art, and make a list. If you are not sure, you can create a list of people and things that you look to often.

DO YOU SEE HOW THEY MIGHT HAVE INFLUENCED YOUR ART STYLE?

WHERE TO START

Finding inspiration is embarking on research. Essentially, you are collecting data on your concept, on its history, nature, and how you will visually communicate the core of your idea.

Research helps to clarify the vision and the goals behind what you are looking for. You gather information that helps you create with confidence and present your audience with a strong work of art.

You don't need to have a fully formed concept to go out and seek inspiration. Furthermore, you can look for inspiration before you even have an idea at all. Maybe you don't yet know what to draw or what your next project will be.

Going out and gathering inspiration is, in a sense, also researching what you will do next. Sometimes I have an idea in mind and possibly I'll have written down some notes and keywords but once I am out at a museum, or I pick up a magazine, I can be drawn to something entirely different and embark on a new trajectory with the idea that just came to me randomly.

Whether you have a concept, are creating from a brief, or just need some visual stimulation, sometimes you might just need to roam the halls of an exhibition or visit a flea market to let your mind wander.

Make sure to take pictures of what stands out to you or calls to you in some way.

WHERE TO LOOK

The fundamentals in chapters 1 and 2, and the activities in chapter 3, can help you to find inspiration for your next art piece or project.

Something that helps me to get inspired is to switch up my routine and try something new. I am definitely someone who searches online for inspiration, but sometimes it's good to get out and about.

DO YOU HAVE ANY INTERESTING PHOTOS FROM YOUR LAST TRIP? WHAT WERE YOU DRAWN TO – INTERIOR DESIGN, HOMEWARES?

TELEVISION

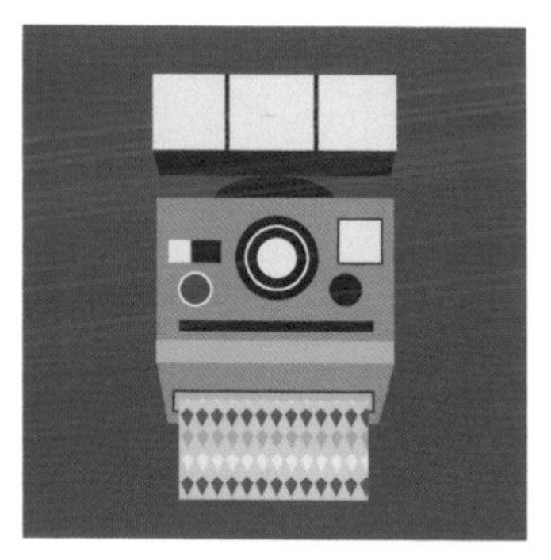

PHOTOGRAPHY

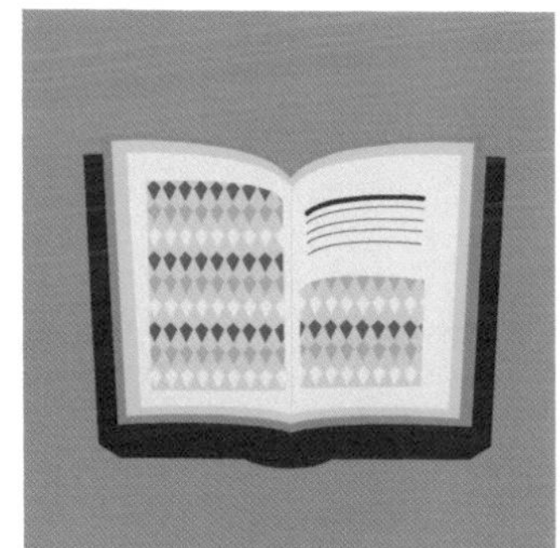

BOOKS

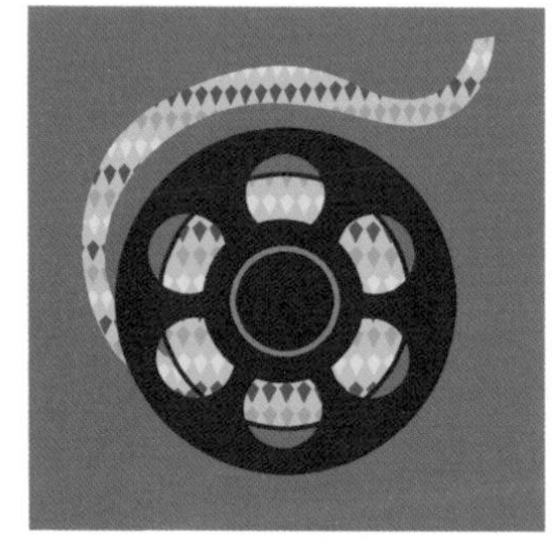

FILM

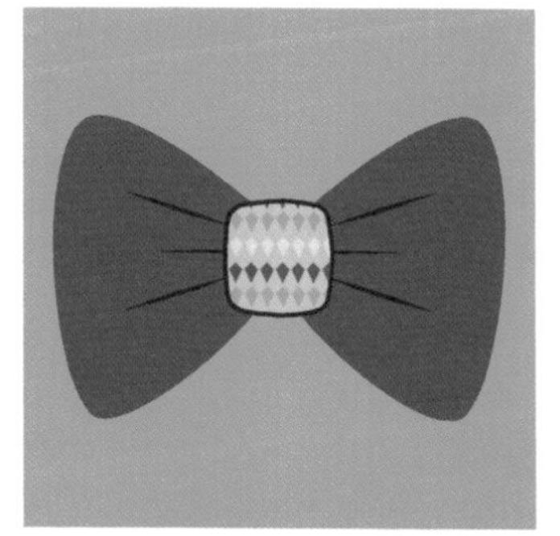

FASHION

MUSIC

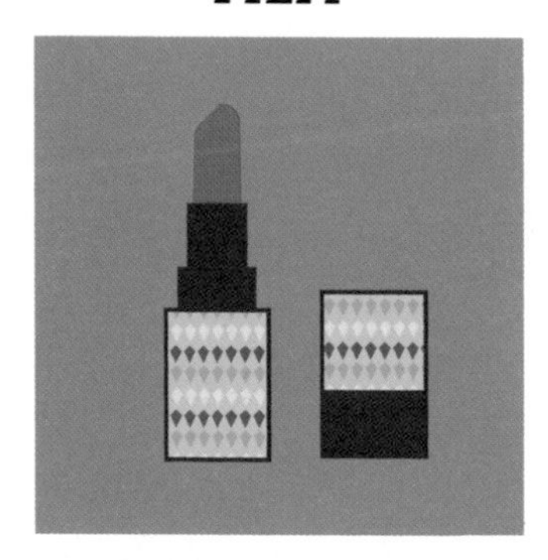

PACKAGING

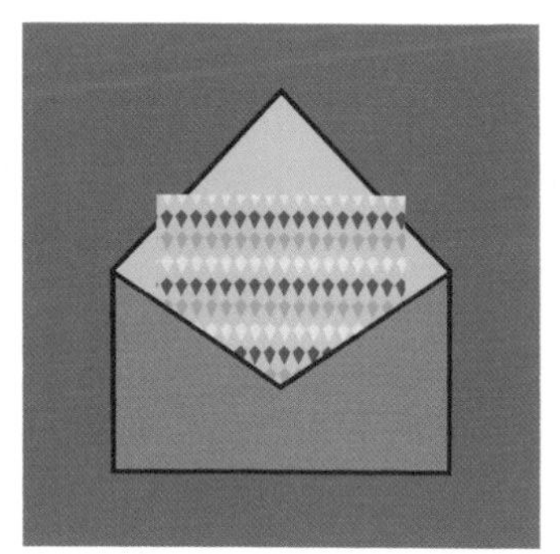

PAPER PRODUCTS

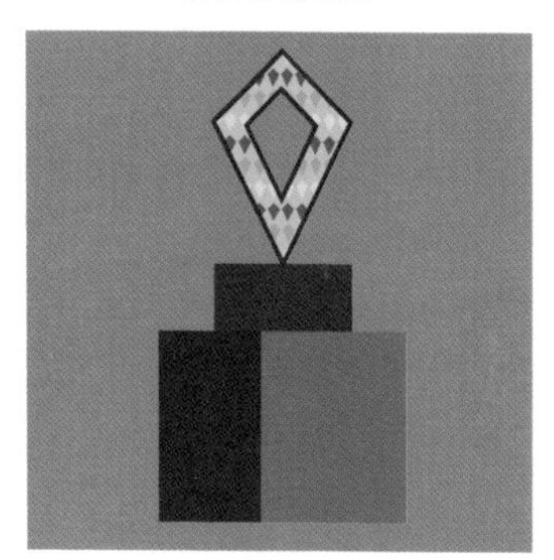

EXHIBITS

NATURE

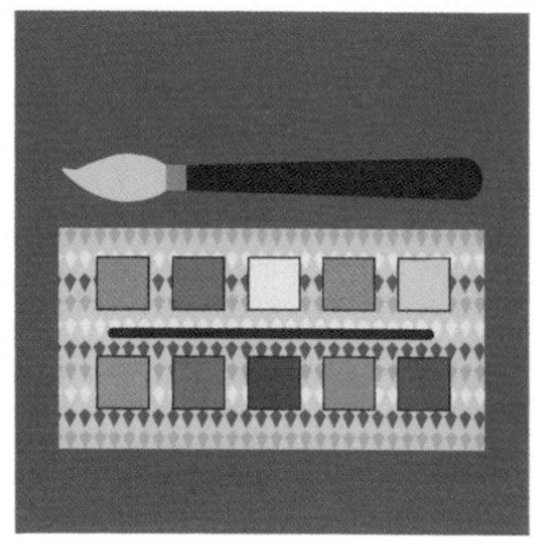

ART

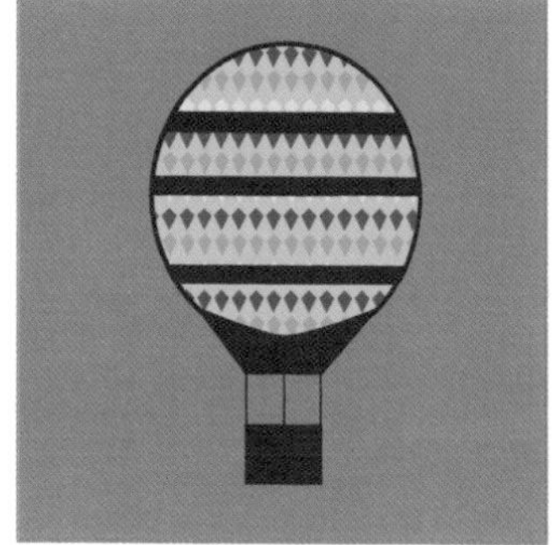

TRAVEL

CREATIVE BRIEF

A **CREATIVE BRIEF** serves as inspiration and an outline of a project. In a professional context, it's often a plan that brings together many stakeholders and provides details on timelines, budgets, and the overall scope of a project.

Writing your own creative brief focusing on key areas can help you to organize your thoughts, build a concept, and create a narrative and ideas around your work.

There are many online resources available that provide creative briefs that can help spark a new idea.

A standard creative brief would include some of the following:

COMPANY NAME
What is the name of the company setting the brief?

COMPANY BACKGROUND
What type of company is it?

TITLE
What is the project name?

OBJECTIVE
An overview of the project's purpose or intentions.

HOW LONG WILL IT TAKE? WHO'S THE AUDIENCE? WHAT'S THE PROBLEM/SOLUTION?

COMPETITORS
Who else is creating the same type of product or providing the same type of service?

TARGET AUDIENCE
Who is the project trying to reach?

LOOK & FEEL
What is the overall mood/experience you would like to convey?

This is a condensed summary of a creative brief – some go into much more detail.

When I create my own creative briefs I keep it simple and short, focusing on the overall objective, audience and look & feel.

I do quick searches on competitors from time to time, but I mainly use a brief to focus my idea and have a guide that I can return to while I'm working through my projects.

MOOD BOARD

A **MOOD BOARD** is collage of images, words, textures, colors, and so on, that helps to visually present a concept or style. They can be physical or digital, for example using slides or image apps. Mood boards can also be created with multiple pages.

In the graphic design field it is not uncommon to have a mood board that represents the overall design, a board for typography, and a board for the target audience, for example.

Some artists also like to highlight different segments within a single board. The sky is the limit on how one can go about creating a mood board.

MOOD BOARDS ACT AS A GUIDE TO VISUALLY EXPLAIN THE IDEA AND OVERALL VIBE OF A PROJECT.

I use a mood board to help me organize the aesthetic and as a reference to check back and see if I am still following my initial ideas.

TREASURE

EXPEDITION

GOLD

MERCHANT

JOURNEY

KEYWORD LIST

OVERBOARD

PIRATE

WHALE

CREW

CARIBBEAN

MAP

SHIPWRECK

PIRATE

SKULL

CAPTAIN'S LOG

NEW FRONTIER

HIGH SEAS

WAVE

PETER PAN

STORM

COMPASS

DESTINATION

KRAKEN

BOOTY

JEWELS

LONG LOST

KEYWORDS are important terms that help describe a concept.

Creating keyword lists is one of my favorite idea-generating activities. I am a huge notetaker and believe that is why I like to work from lists. It is my go-to for brainstorming and brain dumping the thoughts and images I have in my head.

Once I have an overall concept, I like to jot down keywords that come to mind while thinking about that topic. I then go through my list, writing down new words that can be associated with the keyword I am working on.

This process is known as word association. It's a game or a tool that can stimulate creative thought by spontaneously coming up with other words as a response to a specific word.

EXAMPLE

PIRATE ◊ MERCHANT ◊ BOOTY
OVERBOARD ◊ SHIPWRECK
PETER PAN ◊ CARIBBEAN ◊ STORM
KRAKEN ◊ CAPTAIN'S LOG ◊ SKULL

Once you have your keywords, let your mind run freely and see what words you can associate with them. See if you can combine words you have written down to form new ideas.

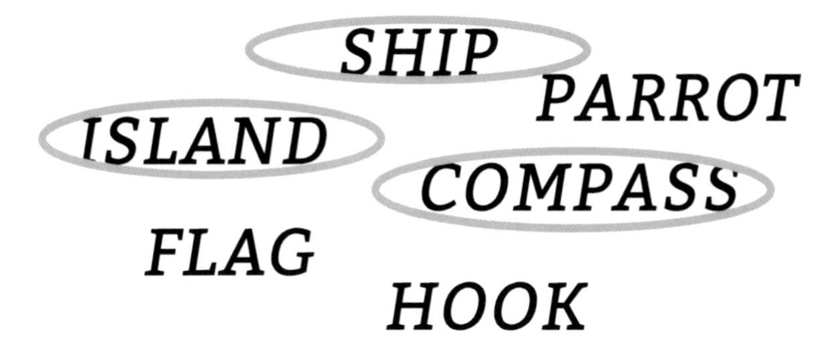

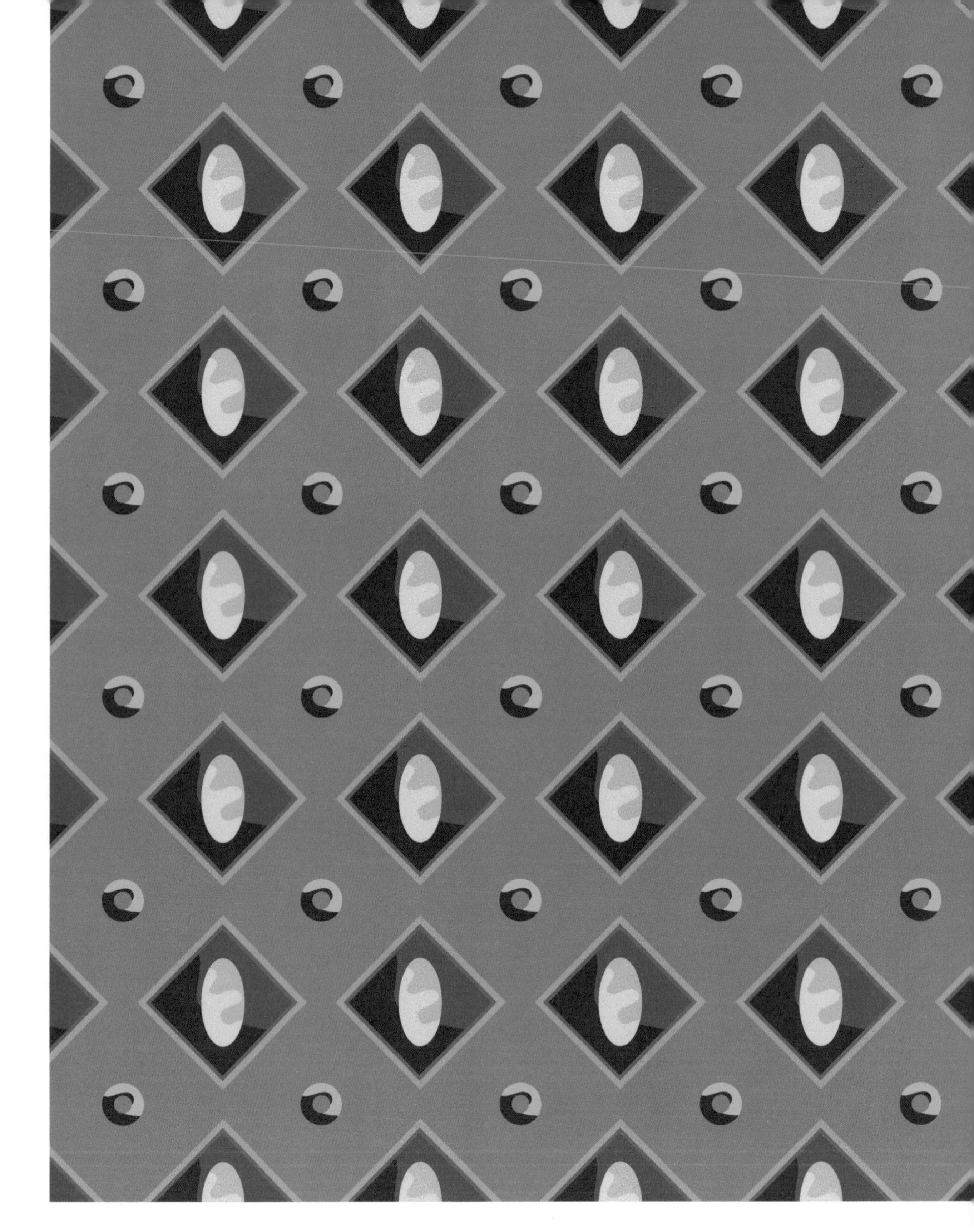

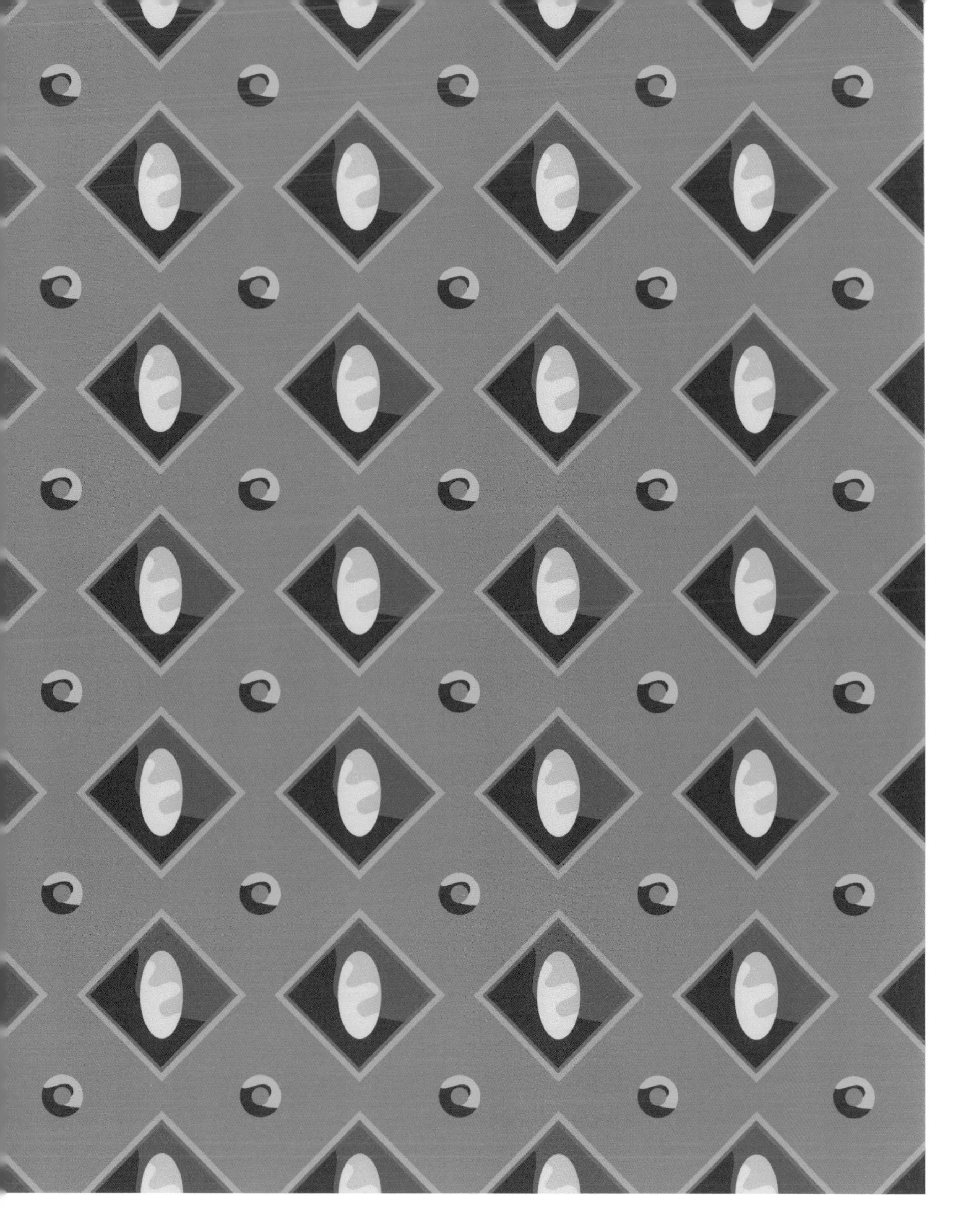

SKETCHING IDEAS

It is not uncommon for me to go through multiple rounds of sketching to ensure I get the proper feel or interpretation of my notes and the images I see in my mind. Though a lot of my work is digital, I still like to sketch out some of my ideas on paper from time to time, which allows me to have an analog practice as well.

Sketching falls into three categories:

- Thumbnail sketches
- Rough sketches
- Final sketches

THUMBNAIL
& ROUGH SKETCHES

THUMBNAIL SKETCHES

These are quick smaller drawings that get your initial ideas down on paper. This is the best way to get all the visual ideas you have for your concept into a sketch before you proceed to develop or finalize any part of your artwork.

You can start to work out basic composition ideas, details, and elements you would like to use in your final piece.

ROUGH SKETCHES

These are the sketches that I do after choosing between one and three different ideas from my thumbnail sketches.

Rough sketches are usually larger, which allows me to start to think about the overall composition. I must admit that sometimes I get carried away with my rough sketch phase and I can end up creating a final sketch.

FINAL *SKETCH*

This is the sketch that will help guide and most likely look closest to your final artwork. This is not to say you won't make changes while drawing your final piece, but it will be the catalyst to start your completed work.

Think of it also as a refinement stage. Just because it might be the "final sketch," you can still explore other possibilities. Who knows – your final sketch might really be your "final, final, final sketch version 2."

Keep your sketches. These are a part of your process, and they can help you see where you need to invest more time in fleshing out an idea or where you need to practice certain drawing elements.

KEEP YOUR THUMBNAIL SKETCHES.

Thumbnail sketches are especially important to keep as they convey different visual solutions for a concept. They can become final artworks for other projects or be used as starting points for new ideas.

These design fundamentals are here to help you start a practice, get out of a rut, or inspire you to experiment and look into different ways to express your creativity.

Before finalizing your piece in color, create a black-and-white version to see if it is balanced.

3

PRACTICE, PRACTICE, PRACTICE

For some of you, the fundamentals might seem like a lot of extra work. I implore you to try out a few, for at least one project or a series.

See what works for you and what you have learned about your art and yourself during the process.

I would like to plant the idea in your mind of understanding art and its creation as a discipline.

Yes, it should be enjoyable and a way to express yourself, but I feel certain that if you start researching, gathering images and ideas, and creating a process unique to you, staring at a blank page will happen less often, and you will see improvements in your work.

There is discipline in following a process, such as drawing multiple sketches before you finalize your design.

With every piece of work you create, you improve your portfolio. With every creative brief and finalized presentation, you have a starting point for conversation to build up your network and your audience.

Trying something new in your work takes a leap of faith to see if it is something that could be adapted and showcased in the long term.

It's taking that art course, watching that video on anatomy, going out on a rainy day to get to the museum because your project calls for it. It's making time for your craft and investing in its future, whether it stays with you as your hobby, as your livelihood, or your dream job.

CREATING ART IS A LIFELONG JOURNEY WHERE YOU DEVELOP AND HONE SKILLS AND CREATIVE IDEAS.

You never stop learning with art, and that might be why I love it so much.

Seeing creativity as a discipline and a lifelong journey should release you from the pressure to do and know everything today.

WHY ART IS CALLED A DISCIPLINE

BUILDING
A ROUTINE

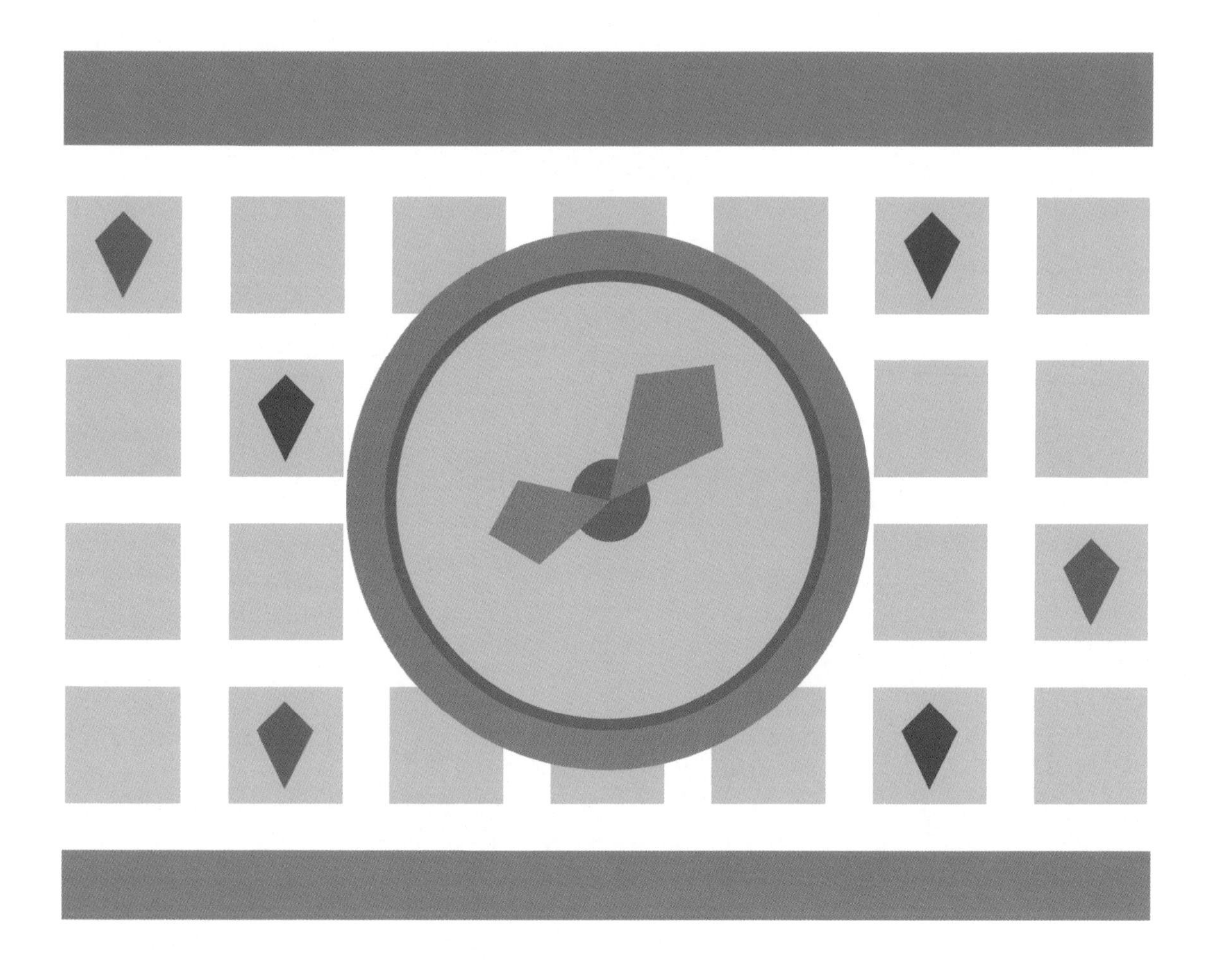

WHAT WOULD YOU LIKE TO CREATE?
Do you want to try a new medium? Go digital? Create work in a series? Do you want to add work to your portfolio based on a certain concept? Would you like to start taking on client work?

With a clear goal in mind you will be able to establish a regular time to practice and a scheduled timeline to complete your projects. This is why having an art process can help you with your work.

If you have a process, you can work on multiple projects at the same time. With a concept and creative brief you can come back to projects at various stages. You might be sketching on one project and going out for inspiration on another.

With a process, you can also establish a timeframe for how long it takes for you to finalize your work.

If you have a different day job, a process can help you set aside time and, most importantly, establish how much work you can take on from clients and how much you will charge.

Of course, there will always be variables, but having a guide for how you work can help ensure you have a way to find inspiration, manage your time, and communicate your activities to clients, galleries, or potential customers.

Establish a timeline for all the steps in your creative process. From there you can determine the necessary time needed for a whole project.

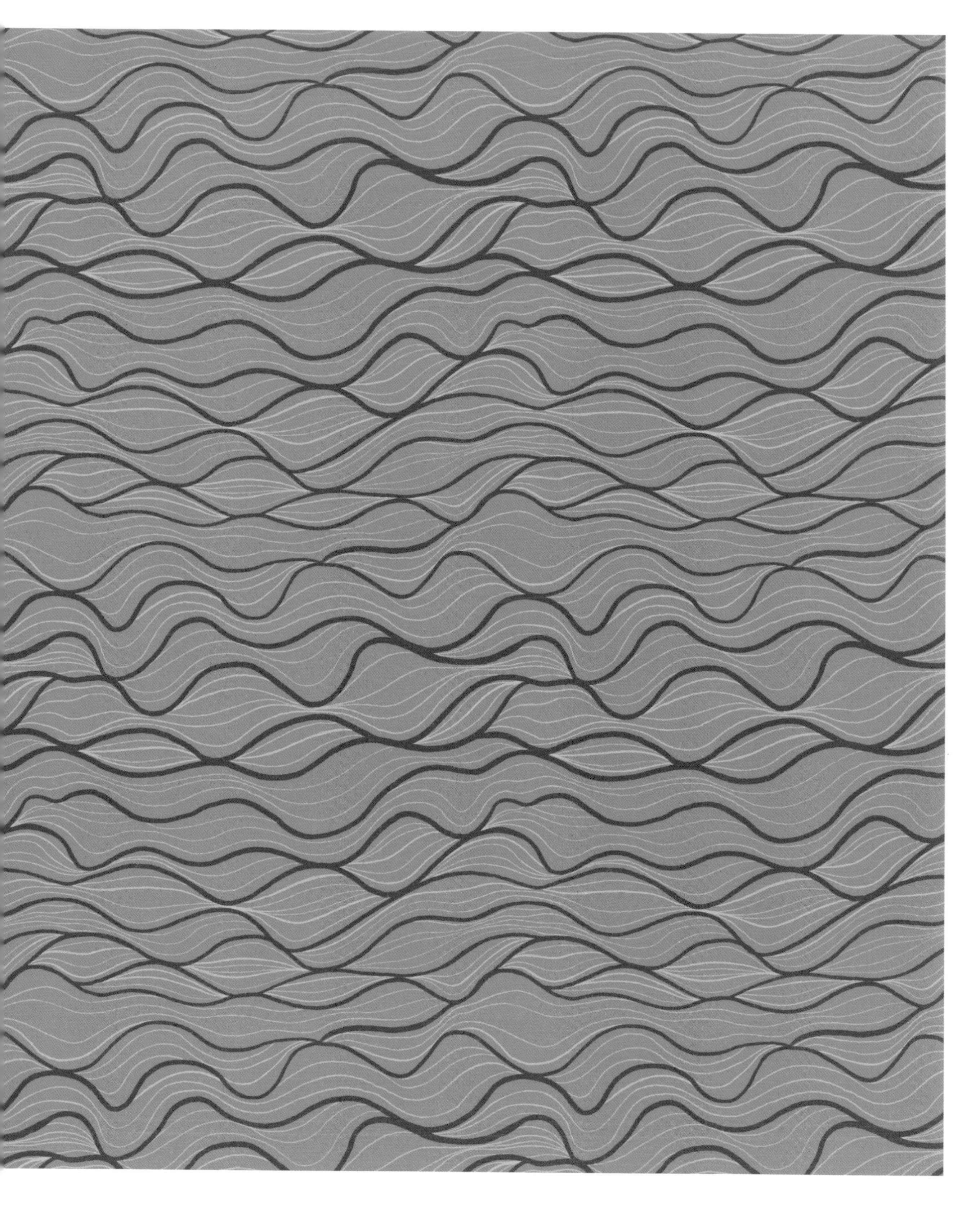

ART
CHALLENGES & CLASSES

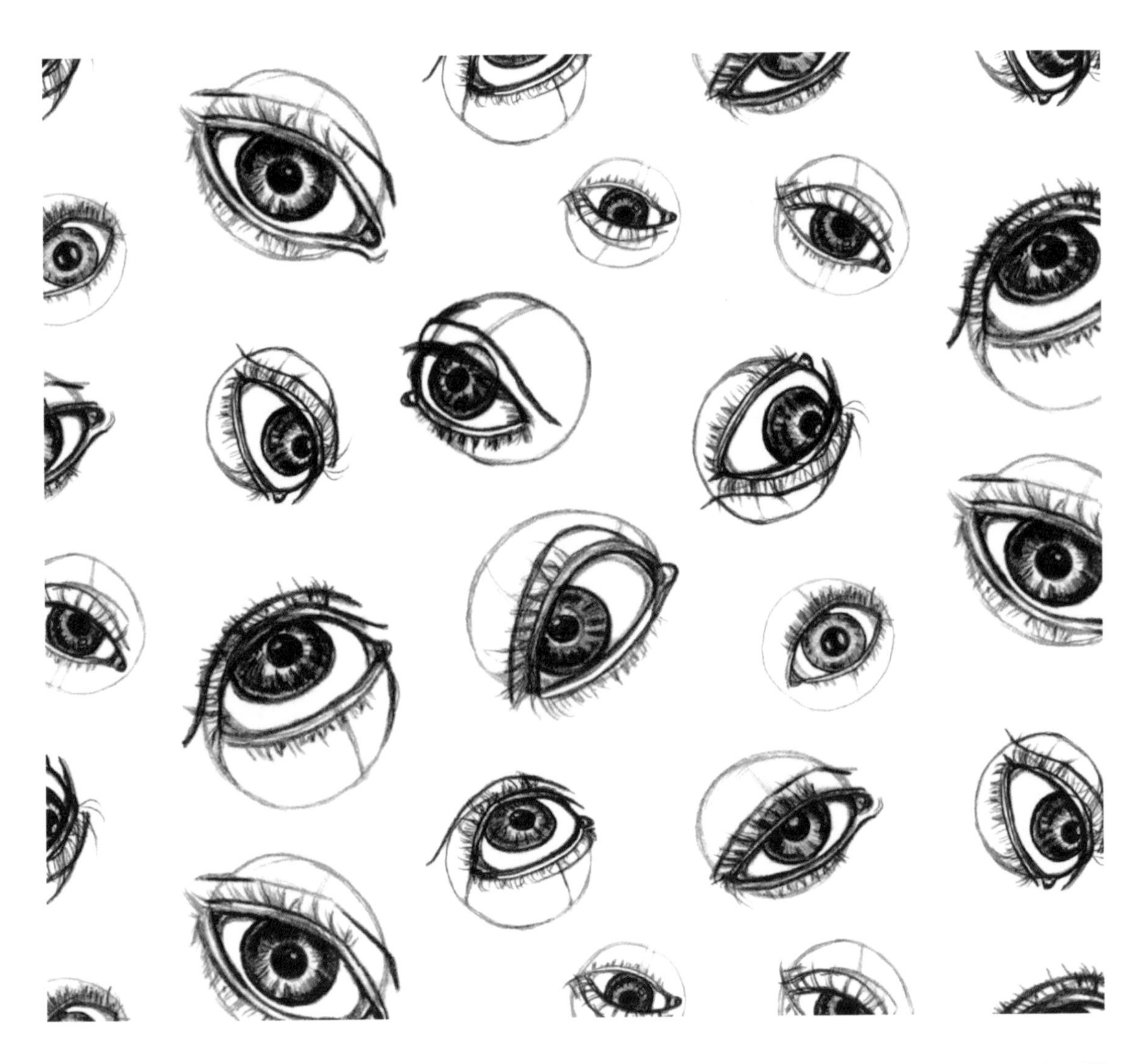

ART CHALLENGES are a fun way to get in practice time. You might take on a challenge that gives specific prompts and your goal is to complete each piece of work in a series.

You might create challenges for yourself based on a number of days or amount of work. Let's say you want to improve the way you draw eyes. You can give yourself a set timeframe to draw 50 eyes from different angles.

This can be done for other subjects as well and there are artists who host challenges on various social media platforms.

ART CLASSES are still a go-to for me. I love that there are so many avenues to learn new skills. Nowadays, you don't have to just take in-person classes or sign up for a degree to learn a skill you are interested in.

With online courses and online learning platforms catering to a wide array of creative endeavors, there are so many interesting things to learn and improve on.

Of course some lessons are better than others, but many are free or low-cost, so it's often worth giving something a try.

I love online courses and through them I have gained knowledge and the courage to write this book. And with all these opportunities to learn and grow in the arts it can be overwhelming to work out where to start, what to do, and what you are good at. That's one of the reasons I wrote this book.

CREATING A PROCESS FOR YOURSELF TO STUDY AND CREATE ON A REGULAR BASIS CAN HELP YOU LEARN NOW AND REACH YOUR GOALS IN THE FUTURE.

If you have been on the fence about a class, it might just be the time to try. Someone once told me that even if a class isn't for you, you learn as much as you need to identify that, and then move on to the next.

COPY
OTHER ARTISTS

I can hear a huge gasp coming from a lot of you. I hear you, but I am not talking about copying as in plagiarizing someone else's art, but rather about using it to improve yours.

Copying other artists can help train your eye to see, and it can help improve your work tremendously.

There is something compelling in seeing an anatomically correct black-and-white sketch and using that to recreate what you see. I use sketches by other artists to help me break down the human features into shapes.

Copying also helps me interpret angles and poses better when I use reference materials.

IT'S ALSO GOOD TO TRACE WORK IN YOUR PRACTICE TIME.

You might think that's an even crazier idea. Hear me out. If I am stuck and can't quite see the angle of a line, the lighting, and so on, then I will trace over the difficult areas. This helps my brain to see the form. I then use a clean version of my reference image and a marked-up reference as visual guides to draw the image anew.

REDRAW
YOUR WORK

Redrawing is one of the activities that helped me improve my work, so much that I could see progress in a short time.

You may be familiar with artists on social media who showcase their work from a year or more previously, and then show their current rendition of the same concept. You can then visibly see progress in line work, anatomical representation, and even in some cases a style shift.

I LIKE TO REDRAW WHEN I WANT TO IMPROVE SOMETHING, OFTEN THE FACE OR THE ANGLE OF A FIGURE'S POSE.

Especially at the beginning of my journey, I would often sketch the same work over and over to train my eye to see better. With each new version, I would see something I could improve that wasn't visible to me before.

Sometimes I would come back a month or months later to work on the same piece and see where I could improve things.

By then I could really see a difference between the versions, which kept me motivated and in a phase of experimentation.

This was my practice: I come up with a design or an idea, create a mood board, sketch a few versions, and then finalize. After that, I would come back and try again after some time passed. Not only did my work improve visually, but I was also able to improve the narrative of the piece by trying more abstract concepts.

On the opposite page you can see the different versions I created for an illustration inspired by the song "Aurora." The fourth image was created three years later; you can see my style emerge and I have added some much-loved pattern design to my artwork.

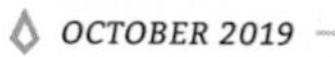
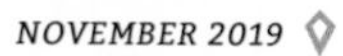

OCTOBER 2019 — NOVEMBER 2019

MARCH 2020 — OCTOBER 2022

REIMAGINE
YOUR WORK

There is no "one size fits all" solution to a concept or design problem. You can explore multiple avenues in your visual communication; especially for those pieces that you complete and wish you'd done differently.

THIS IS WHERE KEEPING YOUR THUMBNAIL SKETCHES COULD COME IN HANDY.

Also, when you rework your art, you might change some details in the new version. Perhaps the original had a hat but then you decide to remove it, or the overall style of it changes.

If you are drawing a certain type of flower or even letters, perhaps the stems or serifs curve differently with each version.

This is also a way of training yourself to use reference material only for certain details and not the whole image. Perhaps it's the coat or the futuristic building that gives you some ideas.

The images shown are inspired by ATEEZ's song "Wave." Initially I took a literal approach to the design and then moved towards a fashion-styled portrait. The final piece has more of the energy of a fantastical story.

SEPTEMBER 2019

OCTOBER 2019 FEBRUARY 2021

CREATING
IN A SERIES

Creating in a series means you create a collection of work with a common concept or theme.

YOUR WORK MIGHT HAVE THE SAME SUBJECT, COLOR, OR TEXTURE, OR CERTAIN MESSAGES YOU ARE TRYING TO CONVEY.

For example, you might like fairytales and want to create work around various characters that have inspired you. You might also have an idea based around a specific place that you want to explore a story for.

When you create in a series, you help convey your concept on a deeper level, and you ultimately have more work for your portfolio. You can start off by creating smaller series of artworks in sets of three or a mini pattern collection telling your story in three main parts.

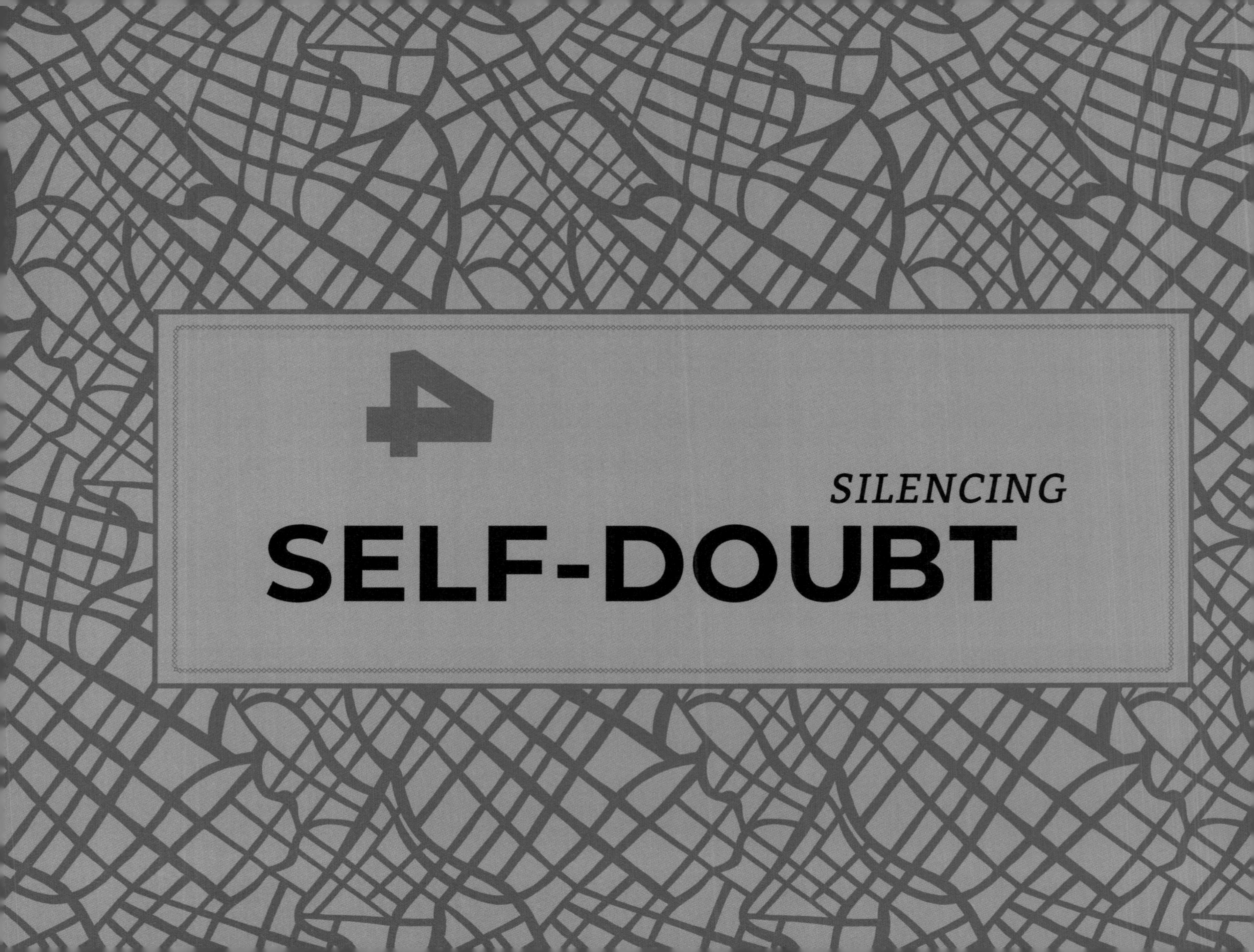

4

SILENCING SELF-DOUBT

IMPOSTER SYNDROME

I once read that the creative industries have the highest rates of imposter syndrome. So, what is it exactly? It's the fear of being seen as a fraud (imposter) due to the doubt of one's successes, talents, and skills.

"DO I HAVE WHAT IT TAKES?"
I think there is always some underlying uncertainty when someone pursues a creative job. This is fueled by the idea of the "starving artist" and, of course, the constant change in activities and need to develop fresh ideas and new perspectives.

"AM I TALENTED ENOUGH?"
"I CAN'T COMPETE!"
As an artist, we are not only putting our work out into the world, but also a bit of ourselves. Art – even graphic design – can be very personal for some and putting yourself out there to be judged can be a scary pursuit.

"WHAT IF THEY DON'T LIKE IT?"
I have come to learn that someone always will, and it should start with yourself – and hopefully your mom and grandmother too.

If you notice you feel like an imposter and it keeps you from creating altogether, it might be best to seek help in addressing the feelings you have and work through what is holding you back.

If taking on that challenge feels like too much right now, or if you're overwhelmed by applying for a job or competition, maybe start small by developing your art process and practice. From there, you can gain experience and confidence, address some of your fears, and slowly work your way up.

PERHAPS YOU FEEL OVERWHELMED BECAUSE YOU THINK YOU NEED TO BE PERFECT IN MULTIPLE AREAS BEFORE YOU EVEN START.

Some skills take time to improve and master. Allowing yourself to see that being a creative is a lifelong journey might allow you to remove some of the pressure to be perfect.

IF YOU MAKE ART, YOU ARE AN ARTIST.

COMPARISON

Let's face it, with social media, cool art books, artistic posters, and street art designs all around us, how can we not compare ourselves?

Believe me, when I first decided to create art again and be an artist, I went through bouts of imposter syndrome, regular comparison, and long periods of procrastination. I was overwhelmed by working out what to create, so naturally I looked to the internet and social media, to see the art that was out there already.

There was a plethora of subjects and artistic styles. I gravitated to a few things in the beginning, trying out various subjects, only to go online and compare what I had created and see if it was "good enough." This, of course, discouraged me and took all the joy out of drawing.

SO, HOW DID I STOP COMPARING MY ART?

I FOCUSED ON WHAT I WAS CREATING.

This took time. But one productive thing I did with some of my comparisons was to write down what I wished I could do better. Maybe it's the hands, the eyes, the hair, and so on. Whatever it was, I made a note, and then I went hunting for study materials to see what I could do to improve.

I LOOKED TO WHAT I REALLY LOVED DOING AND TO MY ARTISTIC INFLUENCES TO HELP GUIDE MY NEW ENDEAVORS.

I know I keep repeating myself. Regular practice with a creative process helped me to focus on what I was doing and what I needed to improve, instead of looking at how I didn't measure up to someone else's work.

What this taught me was that I am unique and have a unique artistic perspective on my subject and concepts. If you focus on you and your work, you will strengthen your skills and develop a style unique to you.

On this journey I'm taking, I have joined art communities in areas such as fashion illustration and surface patterns. Both brought me much joy, knowledge, and more self-reflection.

The biggest takeaway I got was that what I'm doing did seem familiar to some audiences and yet also unique. I combine my illustrations with fully executed patterns. Not fully fashion, not fully surface pattern but **100% ME.**

There was trial and error and, of course, practice, practice, practice. I continued to do my thing even though it didn't fully fit into a specific category.

So it's with this knowledge that I'm writing this book – not comparing myself, but instead fully enjoying other artists' work and wondering "how did they do that" instead of "I could never do that."

›PROCRASTINATION

To procrastinate occasionally is not uncommon, but you don't want to find yourself working on a project and finding that some distraction conveniently comes up, so you end up burning the midnight oil in order to meet your commitment.

Procrastination can become a problem when you put things off for longer periods of time. It's the self-doubt creeping in, or the draining away of motivation to pursue a given project. Habitual procrastination can even hinder you from achieving your art goals and move down a path of self-sabotage.

WHY DO YOU PROCRASTINATE?

I have procrastinated at times, doubting my skills and worrying about the time it would take to master those skills. As mentioned previously, I would compare myself to other artists and wish I was at their level. In some ways, I was diminishing the work they'd put in to get there.

I procrastinated because I feared the outcome wouldn't be what I envisioned, or that I would never be able to work in a creative field in the future.

It was the silent "why bother" making me feel like an imposter, keeping me from progressing and making my way forward.

Don't get me wrong, I am not fully cured, but I have a process in place that ensures I create work and get on with the other activities in my life that need doing.

The two main things that have helped me avoid procrastinating are:

- Scheduling time on my calendar to either create or practice art
- Creating a process to ensure I don't get stuck in the "what should I draw next?" phase

I built a routine, drawing anywhere between three and five times a week. If I draw more or work on other creative business activities, that is a plus.

The lack of skills is addressed by the regular practice times and some of the activities I mentioned above, such as engaging in challenges or redrawing my work.

I stopped comparing myself to others by focusing and creating art based on an active process of finding inspiration, which included, but was not limited to, online resources.

The "why bother" voice began to have a reason: I love art, I am actively creating it, taking time for it and building a portfolio and making my way into a creative field.

MY REGULAR PRACTICE TURNED INTO A PROCESS THAT BECAME MY PURPOSE – MY "TREASURE FOUND."

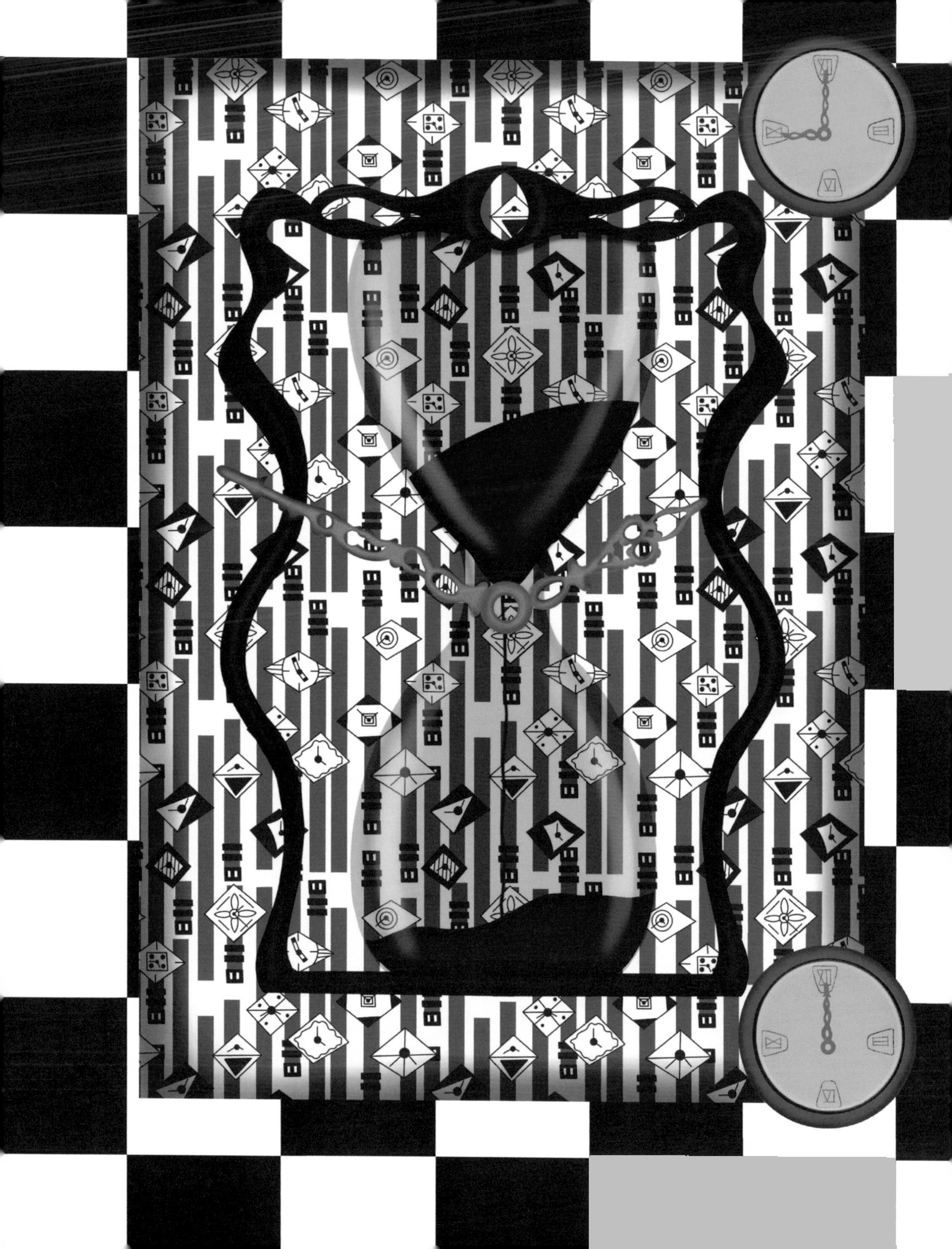

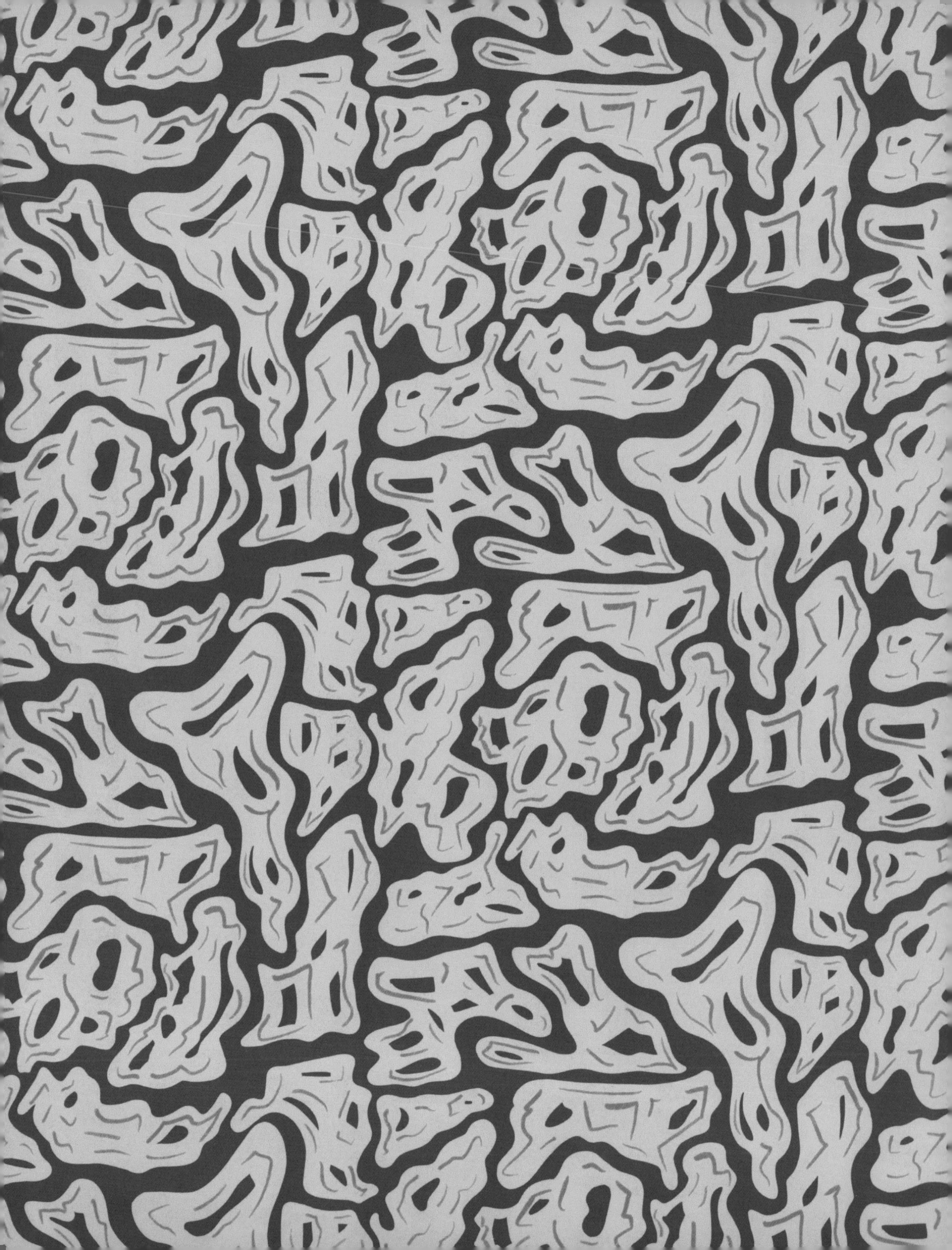

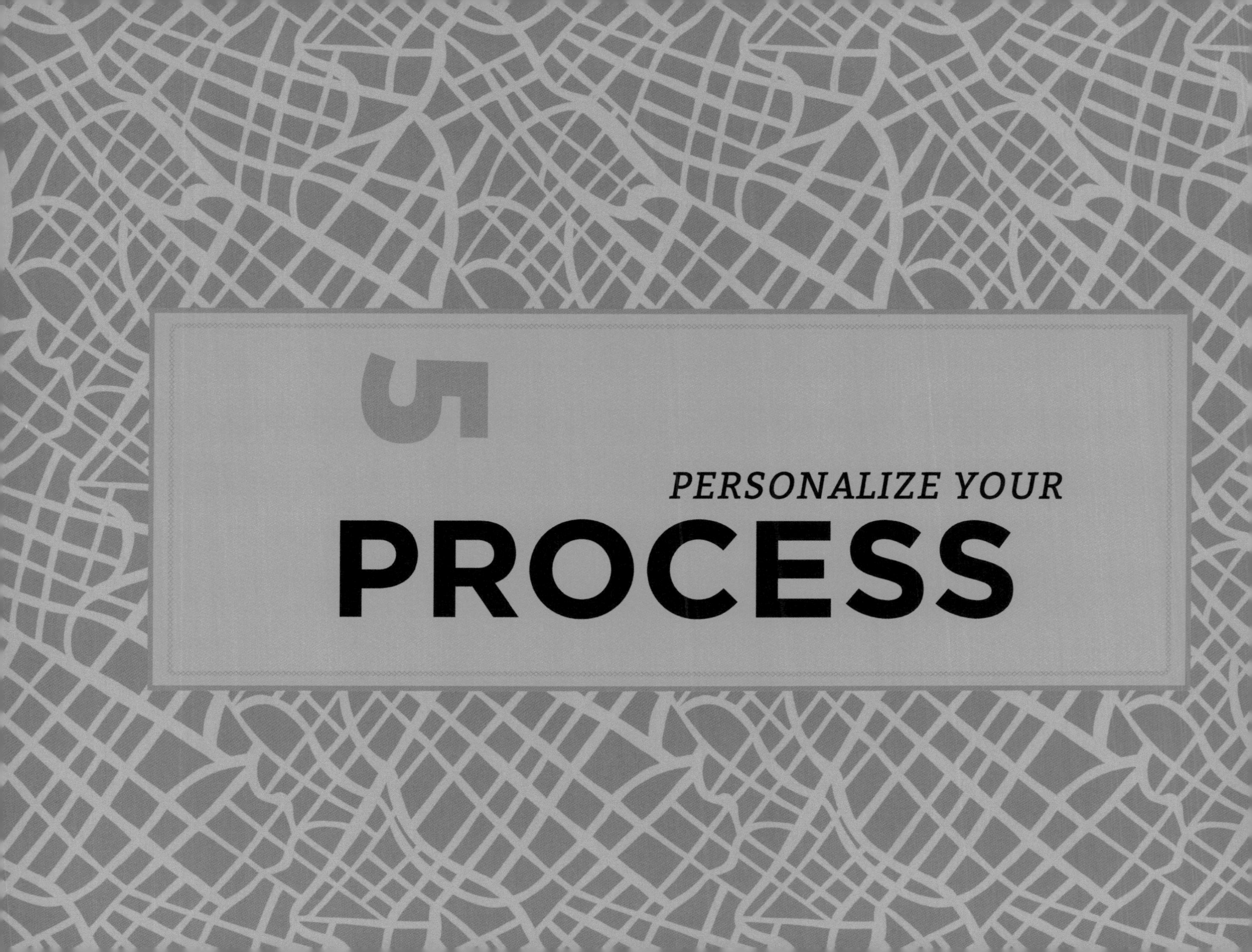
5
PERSONALIZE YOUR
PROCESS

›OUTLINING
WHAT YOU DO

You might already have some go-to activities for when you create a new piece of work. Possibly you go online to search for images, or you sketch analog and then scan to finalize the work digitally. Maybe you work in only one particular medium.

Look at your past work. Do you remember some activities or specific forms of research you did to create your artwork?

We all have a starting point and an end point when it comes to creating our art. Writing down patterns in what you already do can help you to build a process or see that you already have one.

Maybe there is a part of your process you tend to get stuck in, or you don't like doing, but you know it helps your end result. You could reorder some activities, add some that are mentioned in this book, or remove some altogether.

I don't think a process should be set in stone. It can evolve along with the art or you might not follow all the steps that you have outlined for every project.

Depending on the type of project I create, I might follow all the process steps or only sketch an idea and finalize.

As an example, this is one process I follow:

- Keywords and notes
- Creative brief
- Inspiration gathering
- Mood board
- Sketch thumbnails
- Sketch final
- Create digital final
- Create process presentation

Floral Warm
Spring / Summer
Fade Away
Patterned Sweet
Feminine
Colorful

Illustrated Print Ad Campaign

Concept: My Sweet Flower

Company
Made up Bags
Known for their high quality crafted bags with beautiful prints and patterns

Objective
Print Ad campaign showcasing the floral prints & patterns of next spring/summer season bags.
3 Illustrations:
1 illustration showcasing bag on person
2 illustrations highlighting a print

Audience
Made up Bags customers
Illustration and pattern fans

Competitor(s)
Other bag companies in mid-range to high range price category. Other bag companies that focus on prints both embroidered or stamped on to leather.

Look & Feel
Floral pattern with warm to pastel tones
More abstract florals.
Have some of the images fade away through pattern connecting or color blocking.

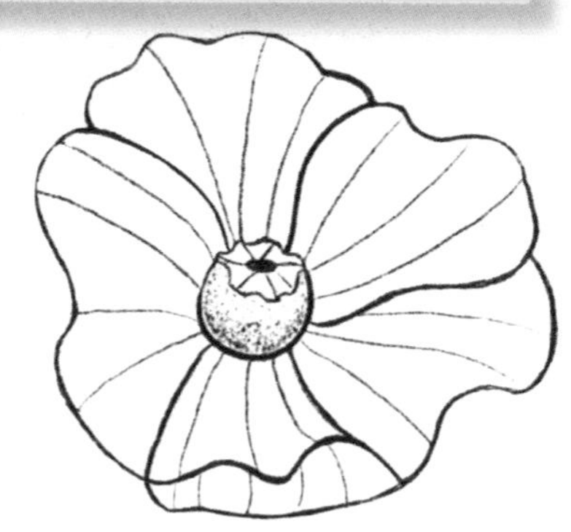

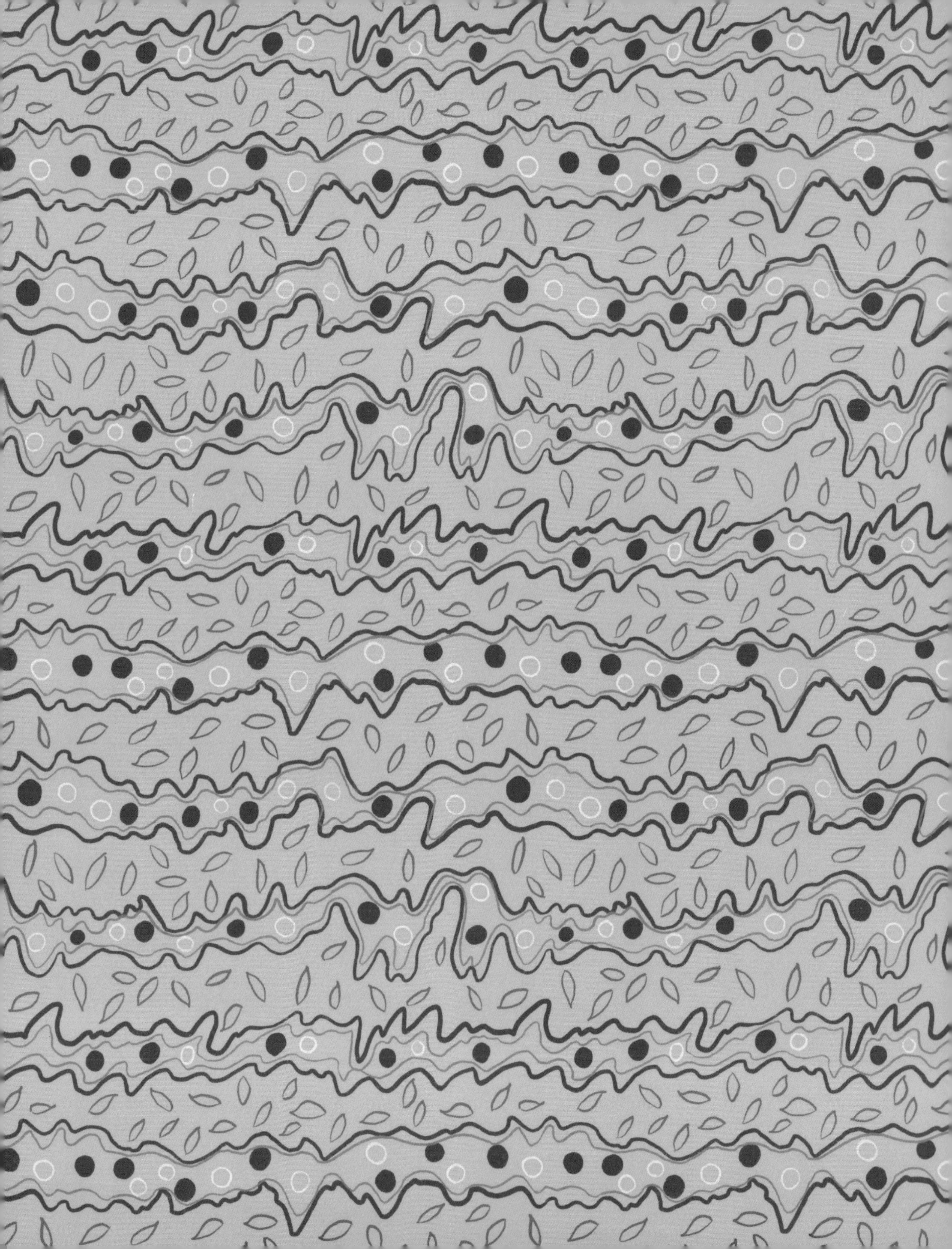

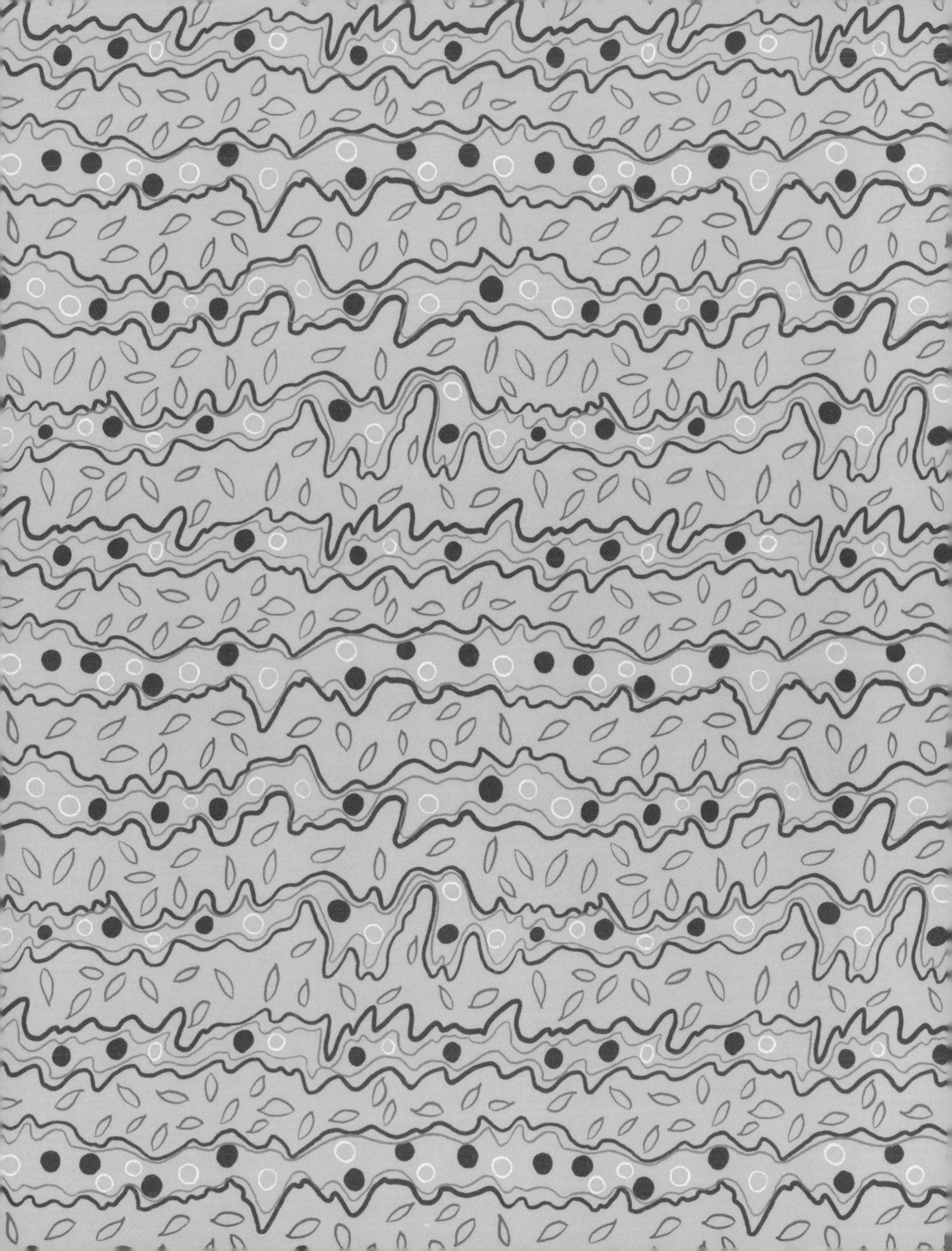

›RECORDING
WHAT YOU DO

Recording your process is part of the process. Keep your notes, files, reference images, and so on, and you can create a presentation that acts as a summary of the design you have undertaken.

Building a presentation highlighting key elements of your process and describing your artwork can be used to pitch projects, communicate to galleries, and explain your execution of a given creative brief.

Your presentation communicates the steps you took in your process from concept to final artwork, acting as the story of the journey based on an idea.

A good way to structure your presentation is to highlight your reasoning and overall process at the beginning, followed by your final design and any additional notes, mock-ups, or instructions on how to handle your artwork.

This may seem like extra work, but if you create templates with the look and feel of your brand or who you are as an artist, you can just drop the key information into your predefined slides and have a quick, clear communication tool to present your artwork.

Even if you don't show a presentation for every piece you create, you'll have a clear foundation and information around your work, allowing you to have a process archive you can refer to for new inspiration.

When structuring your presentation the following can be an idea of what to include:

- Project information
- Creative brief highlights
- Concept and keywords
- Key visual imagery
- Sketches and exploration
- Your final artwork
- Additional notes, mock-ups etc.
- Dimensions and care

Paper Doll Social Club
> Dance
> Soccer
> Photography
> Academics

Fun Bright
Sporty style
Geometric
Community
Vibrant

Mix & Match
>Coming together through fashion
>finding your style

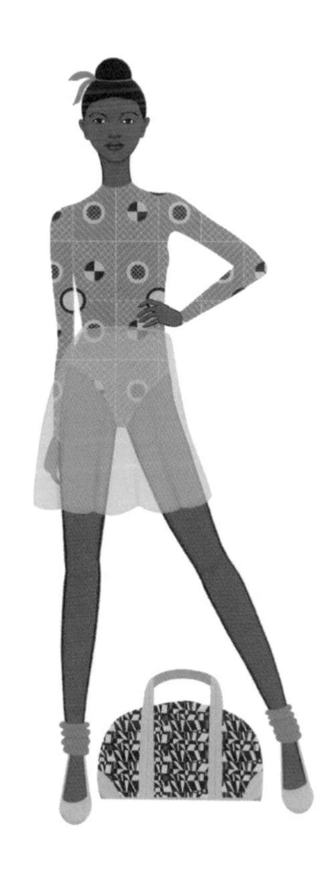

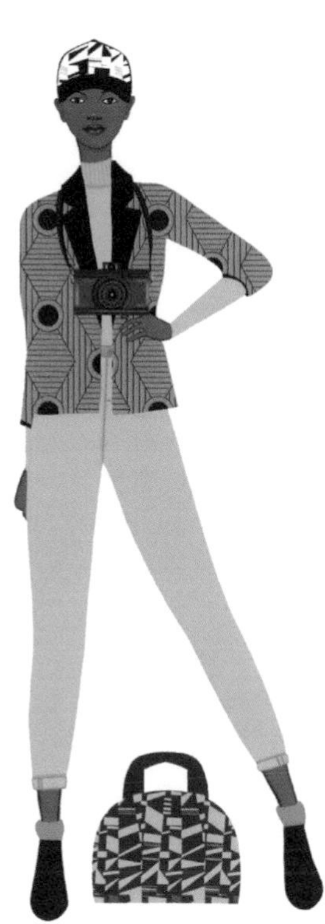

Cinthia James is a passionate creative who illustrates work under the name *A Tale of Art*. She earned her Bachelor's degree in Graphic Design from the Academy of Art University, San Francisco, California.

ABOUT THE AUTHOR

Cinthia currently resides in Berlin, Germany and has lived in the USA and Switzerland. She has developed her skills in illustration and pattern design by establishing an art process with activities to practice and create new work.

Her aesthetic is distinguished by a playful sophistication with the use of vibrant colors and a touch of naivety infusing her subject matter with an eclectic beauty.

Cinthia's work has been profiled in Uppercase's *Surface Pattern Design Guide*.
She is a fashion fan and loves music, especially K-pop, with her number one group being ATEEZ.

THANK YOU

THANK YOU...

...to all those who have supported me through my art journey. To my Oma and Opa who helped make so many of my dreams possible, to my mother for my creativity and my brother for all of the pep talks. And to ATEEZ for their inspiring music and art.

DANKESCHÖN...

...an alle, die mich auf meinem künstlerischen Weg unterstützt haben. Meiner Oma und meinem Opa, die so viele meiner Träume möglich gemacht haben, meiner Mutter für meine Kreativität und meinem Bruder für all die aufmunternden Worte. Und an ATEEZ für ihre inspirierende Musik und Kunst.

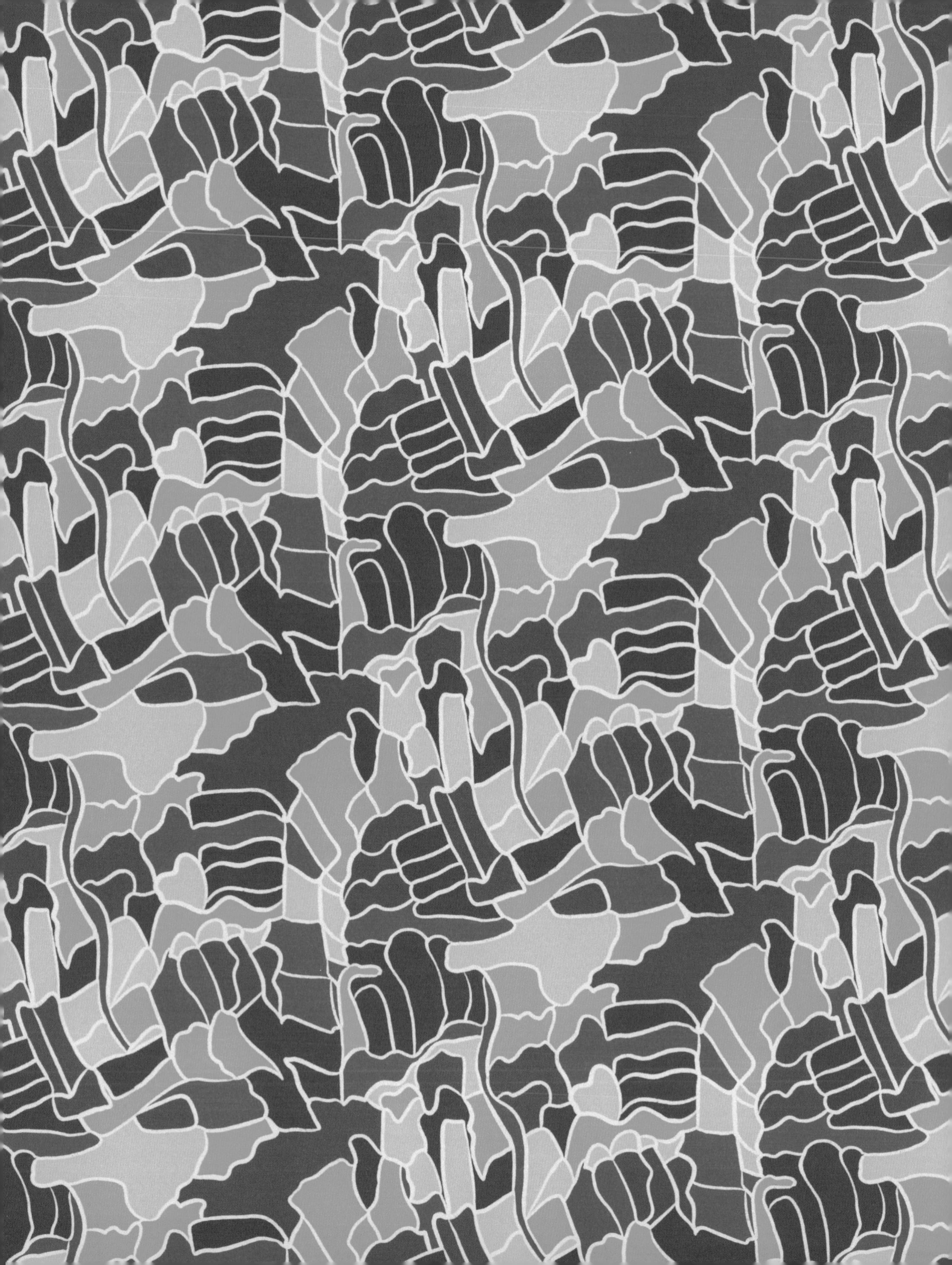

INDEX

ATEEZ INSPIRED

CHAPTER OPENERS

CHAPTER 1
12-13

CHAPTER 2
38-39

CHAPTER 3
72-73

CHAPTER 4
100-101

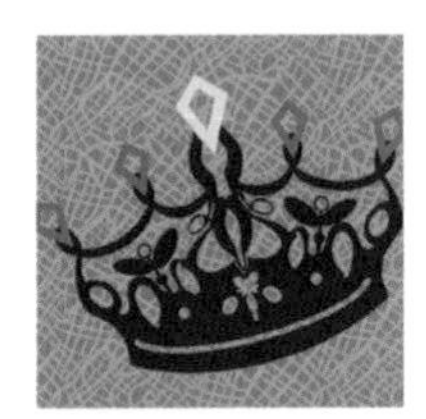

CHAPTER 5
118-119

DESIGN FUNDAMENTALS & OTHER INSPIRED WORKS

BLACK & WHITE 26-27

DARK PATTERNS
102-103

DIAMOND FLORAL
44-45

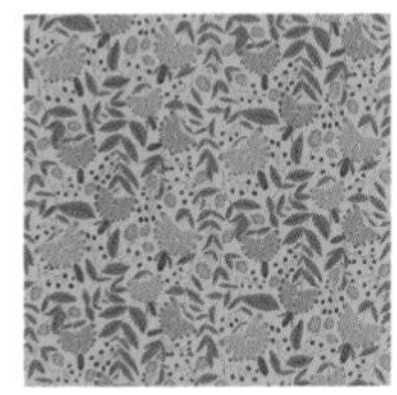

GRID 36-37

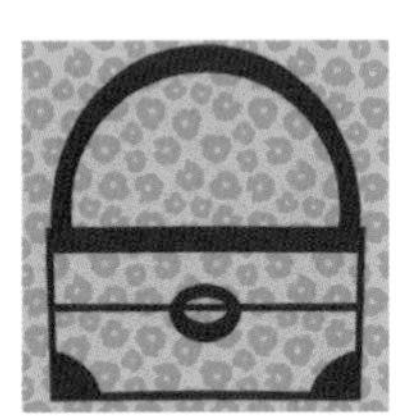

HANDBAGS 124-125

IMPOSTER SYNDROME
104

INSPIRATION 49

LIMITATION 17

NEW WORK 25

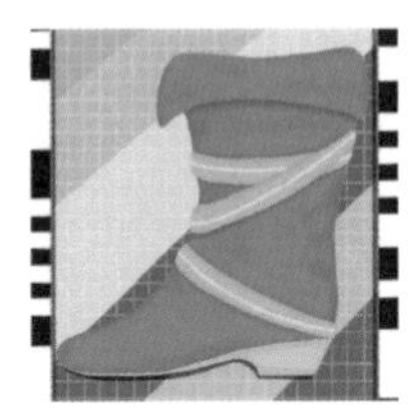

STYLE 28-29

JEWEL & LANDSCAPE PATTERNS

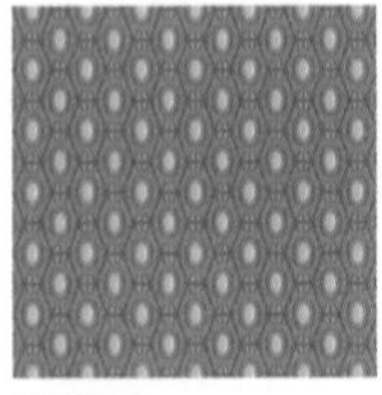

JEWEL 1
14

JEWEL 2
48

JEWEL 3
58-59

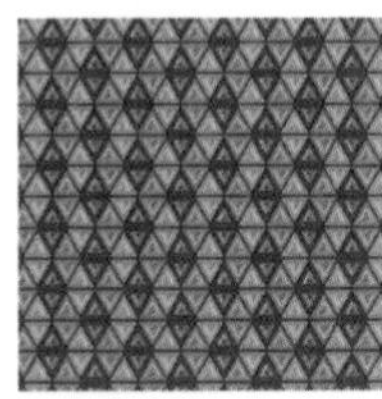

JEWEL 4
76

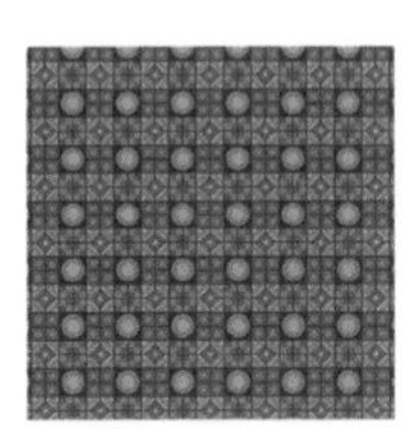

JEWEL 5
77

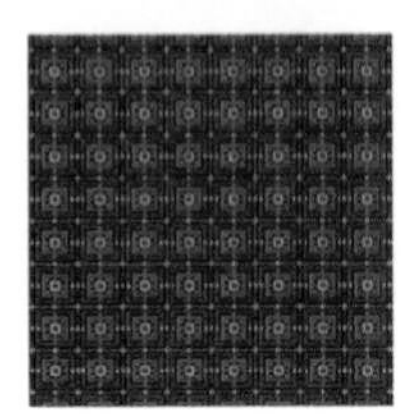

JEWEL 6
102-103

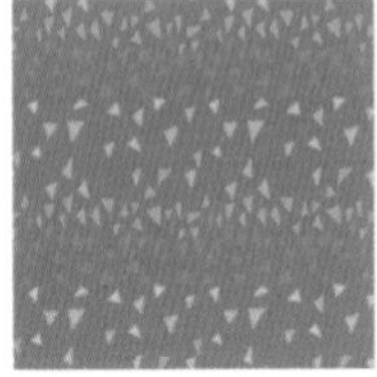

JEWEL 7
132-133

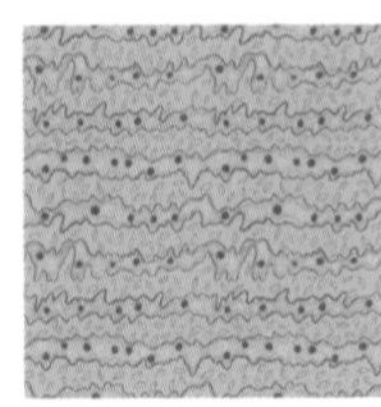

LANDSCAPE 1
126-127

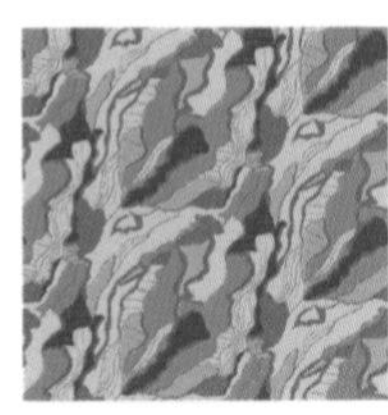

LANDSCAPE 2
40-41

LANDSCAPE 3
42

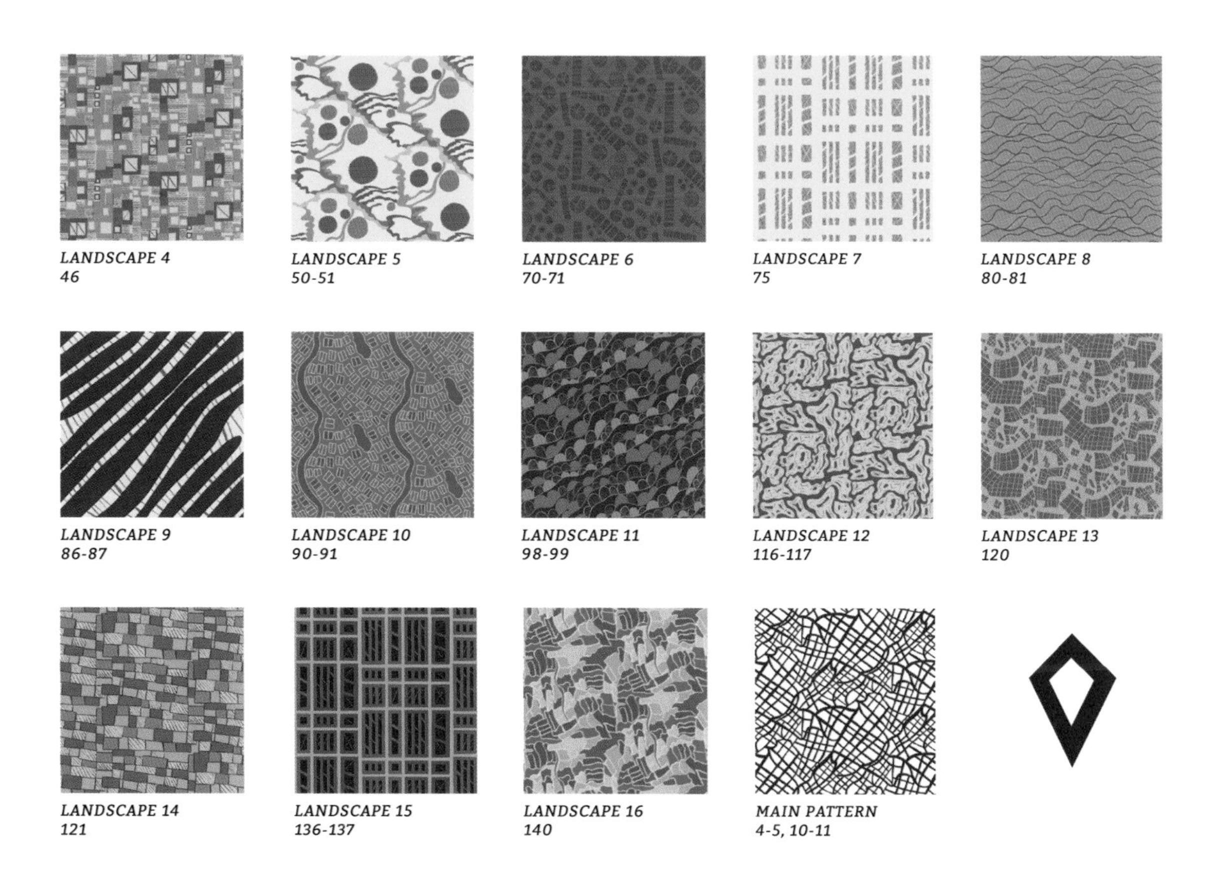

The concept of the book is that of an expedition journal with diamond pins marking the location. Pattern designs following the sub-concepts of jewels and maps (abstract patterns inspired by aerial landscape views) decorate each chapter.

The inspiration gained from ATEEZ was incorporated into the book design and various illustrations within the chapters. I either wrote out keywords from lyrics or reimagined ideas based on the visual imagery ATEEZ showcased in their various "comebacks" (as new releases are known in the Korean music industry).

Printed in Poland
by Amazon Fulfillment
Poland Sp. z o.o., Wrocław